SELLING
By Default

A realistic, honest, and helpful
conversation regarding the profession
of selling

Randy L. Hess

Publishing

Visit my website at www.randylhess.com

Printed in the United States of America

First Printing: June 2010

ISBN- 978-0-615-37382-9

This book is dedicated to my family and friends. They understand this profession, as well as support me unconditionally each and every day.

I also want to acknowledge those individuals that I have met throughout my career. The individuals that notice and appreciate honesty, integrity, and character. You are the ones that have inspired me to put down my thoughts on paper so others might understand what it means to represent an organization as a professional employee.

Liz and Craig —
Best wishes and
hope to meet you
sometime in person!

Table of Contents

Introduction

You are about to read through a conversation about the profession of selling.

If you are new to a selling occupation, or a seasoned veteran, you should find the material worthwhile as well as entertaining.

I'm always amazed at what I hear from people whenever we discus my career.

"Oh, I could never do that job. I just don't have the 'gift for gab.'"

Another familiar comment, "You have to be so outgoing. I just don't like talking to people."

And the last one I will mention, as it is one that I still hear a lot. "How do you deal with all of the travel? I'll bet you miss being at home."

Here are the responses that I usually give to those comments.

I don't have the "gift for gab." In fact, when I'm home at night, I am the last one to pick up the phone, and many times I will ignore it. I really don't go out of my way to start a conversation with a stranger either.

Regarding the travel? Either you like it, and accept it, or it's not for you. I happen to like it. I honestly feel that you will not be successful in a "travelling" sales career if you miss your own bed every night. However, there are plenty of sales jobs out there that require no travel.

Please understand that the material in this book is information based strictly on my opinion. I have a rather independent, entrepreneurial viewpoint and it's not for every person. It is my interpretation based on my beliefs. My mission statement is that it is my job as an individual representing an organization to work closely with my customers and become part of their team. It is to open up avenues for my organization to work closer with them.

The lessons that I have learned as well as the opinions I have formed, may be helpful to others. The purpose of this book is to offer some guidance to someone that may find it appropriate.

I sincerely hope that you enjoy your reading!

CHAPTER ONE

Les Brigham had a lot on his mind this morning.

It was starting to appear as if the sales slump that he had been experiencing was starting to fade. His numbers were starting to increase quite dramatically and this did wonders for his outlook.

Les was also making some real progress with his boss.

Dirk Youngblood was a young, no nonsense director. It had appeared to Les and his fellow teammates that Dirk was too focused on what his upper management team was dictating, and not thinking on his own. They all viewed Dirk as a high strung puppet that danced every step by the tone of the corporate music.

Until recently that is.

Although Les will never take credit for it, he was instrumental in changing the thought patterns of the hard driving Youngblood.

A few months back Les was at the bottom of his pack. This was unusual for Les, as he had been a sales leader for years, most of which were working for a competitor. He had also created a reputation within the ContainPro organization as a mature, respected team leader focusing on how he could benefit the organization by example and focus.

Les was also starting see his motivation being jeopardized by comments and attitudes directed toward him by his management team. He couldn't understand why he and his sales team were being treated like they were a liability rather than an asset. This type of communication was not normal to Les and he decided to do his part in changing the morale of the ContainPro sales team.

After months of negative comments and counter productive correspondence, Les had enough. He walked into Dirk Youngblood's office one morning and started a conversation with Mr. Youngblood that's outcome was as much of a shock to Les as it was to Dirk.

Les essentially restated why he came on board with ContainPro. During that restating process, Les was surprised to find out that Dirk was not exactly happy or confident in his position as well.

Les has a way of interacting with people. That is one of his many core strengths. With Dirk's voluntary admittance of his personal concerns, the two men decided that if they created a plan to work together amongst the whole sales team, a larger degree of success could be achieved.

Now though, Les's current concerns were probably more unique than the normal ones that the other salespeople were dealing with.

Les and Cindy Brigham had recently been offered a rare business opportunity.

An ex coworker of Les's had been running his father-in-law's diversified, multi-faceted business for the past 2 years. When Frank Winman's father-in-law passed away 2 years ago he and his wife Sarah stepped up to the helm of Layman and Son's, Inc.

Herb Layman, Frank's father-in-law had three children. Richard, Rodney and Sarah.

A few years back Rich and Rod were arrested and put in prison for trafficking drugs and guns. They covered up their illegal business under the mask of a high dollar boat reseller.

When they were indicted, Herb disowned them both and changed his entire will, as well as his personal and business estate to his only daughter Sarah. He kept the name of the business the same merely to maintain continuity with his offshore accounts.

Frank and Sarah now had more money than they could possibly spend in ten lifetimes and wanted to enjoy the special lifestyle that was available to them. Managing a small but very lucrative business empire was not viewed as part of that lifestyle. With Frank's age and health the clock was ticking for both he and Sarah.

Les Brigham had recently found Frank at the helm of Layman and Son's when he dropped in on a cold call. Frank and Les were very close and long term senior team mates on the sales force for Morphics, Inc, a very strong competitor of ContainPro.

When they reconnected it was as if time had stood still. Frank always knew of Les's flawless character and work ethic. So he felt Les and Cindy could benefit from he and Sarah's windfall as well. It was as if a missing puzzle piece had been provided when Les walked in the door that day.

There was a lot to digest for the Brigham's. Les would have to end his career as he knows it today and become an immediate CEO of a very diversified company. Les's parents owned a small business while he and his brother were growing up, but nothing of this magnitude.

Les's dad managed a sales territory for a large hardware chain. His parent's owned a Laundromat and Les's mom managed it while raising her two children.

This particular business venture that Les and Cindy were moving toward was obviously much different, and the circumstances surrounding the venture were quite unique as well. It was a different time of life for the junior Brigham, as well as a different economic atmosphere.

The Brigham's children were all grown up and their youngest child Ginger had just moved out on her own. They were true empty nesters and were concerned how they were going to deal with that change in their life.

"Hey Les, you got a minute?" shouted the voice of Dirk Youngblood, across the sales area of cubicles.

"What is it Dirk?" Les responded as he walked toward him.

"I want you to meet Jerry Feldman, he is one of our new sales trainees, and he will eventually be taking over Ken's territory when Ken retires."

"It's nice to meet you Jerry. I'm Les Brigham."

"If you have time this morning, I would like to sit down with both of you. Les, I would like to have Jerry co-pilot a sales trip with you. I was thinking that maybe a trip up north."

This request was welcomed by Les as he really enjoyed the thought of working with new people. But more than that, he enjoyed sharing his beliefs about the selling profession. Les had just started to become much more satisfied in his position with ContainPro as well as working with Dirk. Now with Jerry he had a student that he could help mold and impart his knowledge on. With the recent developments this may be a short lived task.

Dirk motions for both of them to come into his office and he shuts the door.

"Les, you know how I respect your methods. Even though we will be grooming him for Ken's territory, I would like you to be the one that shows him the ropes. Jerry has sales experience, but limited to inside sales, and in the sporting goods industry. He hasn't had an outside position, but that is his aspiration. During the interview process we were convinced that Jerry has many of the traits to be a successful road warrior like most of you. We're going to keep him inside for about two months to absorb as much product knowledge as he can get crammed into his brain. Then we're going to turn him loose and let him keep up Ken's momentum."

"Wow, are you sure about this kid?" Les smirks and then chuckles.

"It's lonely out there, and you have to be self-sufficient. Can you do it?"

"Oh yes," is Jerry's simple response.

"Dirk, I have a couple of urgent phone calls to make, and finish one report. Could the three of us get together in about 45 minutes?"

"Sure, I'll take Jerry over to the manufacturing side and let him get a view of how things get put together. I'll introduce him to some folks. Then maybe we will walk through the warehouse. Let's meet back in my office in about an hour."

"That sounds good." Les says, as he shakes Jerry's hand again.

"See you guys then."

Just a short time later Dirk pokes his head in to Les's cubicle.

"Les, I just wanted to tell you that I realize a couple of months inside before we turn a guy out in the street is probably too soon. However, I'm trying an experiment with Jerry. You've convinced me that sales are predominately about relationships and serving customers. That is what I want you to instill in Jerry. I'm going to be so excited to watch the results. He's green as grass, and you have a blank canvas to develop a first class guy."

"Wow, this is a great opportunity." Les replies.

"Keep in mind, you don't have to work with Jerry if you don't' want to, and it certainly isn't your job to train the new guys. I just have a lot of respect for how you do things, and I want you to have an opportunity to start the design process on this new guy. I will help and oversee everything as well. Let's see if we together have what it takes to start creating some magic. Are you OK with that Les?"

"I'm cool with that," Les responds. "I'm excited to be part of this development team for Jerry." While hearing the words, he knows that the future is going to change dramatically very soon.

"I know you are. Thanks."

Shortly after Dirk leaves Les's cubicle, Les starts to make plans and agenda's. He reviews his upcoming call routes, and decides where his time with Jerry will be best spent.

The three guys get together in Dirks office just as planned. The anticipation is electrifying and optimism is flowing.

"Les, what are your thoughts so far as how we should proceed?" Dirk asks. "It will be interesting if your ideas match mine?"

"Guys, here are my thoughts. I can take Jerry with me most anytime. For the next month I will have a good mix of accounts, established and new, as well as small accounts, and some of my big hitters. However, before we go hit the street, I would like to give Jerry some homework which will make our time together better spent."

"Wow, homework, it's been a while." Jerry responds.

"What type of homework Les?" Dirk asks.

"Just research a few personal thoughts but nothing dramatic."

Dirk and Jerry both express a curious expression.

"I want to know what Jerry wants to accomplish in a sales position. I want to know why he is interested in pursuing this career, as well as his mental time frame toward learning the industry. I realize that you guys went over this in the interview process, but I want to have Jerry build his future plans on the way he feels now."

Dirk is feeling fairly smug right now, not just for hiring someone that appears to be trainable, but also for asking Les to be a key facilitator to Jerry's learning experience.

Les continues. "I also want to know who Jerry knows that has been in this profession or industry. I am interested in his viewpoint as to what kind of people we are."

"Wow Les, I feel like I'm going to be spending time with a shrink. Do you suppose you can get me to avoid sweets and lose some weight while you're at it?" They all laughed.

"I may even give you some specific questions to work on before we embark, but just think about those for now." Les adds.

"Could you keep him inside for the next 2 weeks Dirk? That will give me time to put together a productive outline and make our time worthwhile. A lot of this proposed time will be in a car watching the road move under us. It's a good time to make worthwhile notes and create solid plans."

"That's not a problem Les, I can have him work in shipping for a few days, then move him around to different departments. I think that I will have him hang out with Ken Burris and Luke Stace in the city a couple of days. He can pick up some of the lingo with them while he is waiting for you to take him."

"Perfect. Those are great guys, and they would welcome the chance to help out as well."

"Jerry I would suggest that you bring plenty of notepads along and do nothing but write while listening. When Les gets started, you will want to grab as much information as you can. Sometimes he will even take a breath." Dirk states with a smile.

The anticipation shows in Jerry's face. He is excited and ready to start working for this organization.

Les walks over to Jerry and puts his hand on his shoulder.

"Jerry, I'm going to tell you something. You are going to learn a ton of stuff, and I hope you make good notes. We're going to make you a success."

"Thanks, I appreciate that."

They both smiled and Les headed back to his cubicle to gather his agenda and start his calls..

Chapter One

CHAPTER TWO

The time passed quickly for Jerry. He had worked in three different departments in the company, and had picked up a great deal of preliminary knowledge.

Jerry was a thinker as well. He certainly wasn't lazy, and his goal was to learn as much as he could, and find ways to make a difference for the company. Coincidental enough, it was similar to the principles that Les Brigham held to as a younger man as well, and even today.

"You ready to get on the road rookie?" Les asked Jerry as he was discussing the week's agenda with one of the other salespeople.

"Absolutely Mr. Brigham!" Jerry responds.

Jerry is leaving his car in the company parking lot for the days he is travelling with Les.

"I'll go grab my luggage and meet you at your car."

"Right on, I'll see you out there."

The two men loaded up their material and temporarily organized the cockpit of Les's car. Final check to be sure they had phone chargers and plenty of notepads. Les secured his laptop computer and did one last check in the trunk to see if he had forgotten any sample packs of material. He knew he was stocked, but Les always felt better after one more visual inspection right before departure.

It was a mild spring morning. The trees were starting to blossom in the surrounding suburbs, and you could smell the blooms from some of the surrounding trees and flowers. After the long cold and wet winter, it was nice to experience this annual message from the seasons, that life was about to resume and fun outdoor activities were just weeks away.

Jerry Feldman was a young guy in his late 20's. He had a look in his eye that he was on a personal mission to become a positive standout amongst his coworkers whoever they happened to be.

His dad was an ex regional manager for a large sporting goods chain. Jerry grew up learning about outdoor recreation and all of the new and interesting paraphernalia that his fathers company distributed. He was the younger of two boys in his family.

Jerry's older brother Chris, struggled with life in general, and had taken some tragic turns in his adolescence. As a role model, Chris was little help. Chris was a social icon in school. He had a circle of friends growing up that lead him down a bumpy trail of unclear reality. Alcohol and drugs at a young age pretty much sapped Chris of any drive he had to form a plan for his life. Always short on money, and in trouble with the local authorities, Chris caused a great deal of pain and concern for his parents. Jerry witnessed this growing up, and decided early that he wanted something better for himself. He also felt that it would be a help to his parents if he took a more positive path than his brother Chris.

"So Jerry, how have things been going the past couple of weeks?" Les asked.

"Not bad Les, I've enjoyed the time and the diversity that has kept me busy lately. However, I'm glad to be getting out on the road with you this week. I don't like being cooped up in a building all day. I really need to be moving around more. Routine activities within the confines of a building drive me crazy. The two days out with Ken and Luke were like recess in grade school."

"I know what you mean buddy. I think it's a mindset that we create for ourselves. We either are 'inside people' or 'outside people' and we definitely know where we are happiest."

"How did you happen to get hired at ContainPro?" Les asked, but knew the answer.

"I just answered an ad that a recruiter had placed in our local newspaper. Even though I know nothing about the Industrial Supply business, the thought of being out on the streets representing a reputable company has always appealed to me."

"You didn't like the sporting goods industry?" Les inquired, allowing Jerry to elaborate a bit.

"It wasn't bad. I worked for a company that was one of my father's larger accounts. They knew him and he kind of got all of the puzzle pieces to fit for me to get hired. It was a good company with a great group of people, but I just needed to do something different. Sporting goods was just 'too familiar' for me, and I felt that I would burn out. Dad was well known in that industry, and I wanted to be someone else other than Ted Feldman's kid. Besides, the days of sitting at a telephone and being locked up inside all day drove me out of my mind."

"Again, I know exactly what you are saying."

"By the way Jerry, did they offer, or did you receive any formal sales training with your last company?"

"Yeah, every once in a while, they would have us watch a video, or they would have some dude come in wearing an expensive suit and a flashy watch. He would talk to us about projecting a professional image, and how to increase order volume by suggesting other products. I listened to most of the applicable stuff, and tuned out the crap that I felt was just phony."

"By the way Les, Dirk sure holds you in high regard."

"That's good to hear. He has certainly has had his battles to deal with. It's not easy being a Division Sales Manager for an organization the size of ours. Lot's of people pulling you in different directions. It can be tough. But, that is a whole other conversation."

Jerry listened intently. "Well, he sure thinks you are the model person to train me. It sounds like you have some long term experience in this organization. How long have you worked for ContainPro?"

"About 3 years with this company, but my history and development was with a competitor called Morphics. You'll run into them everywhere, and they could develop into 'dinner table' conversation if you're not careful. They are a good organization as well, just not the company that they once were. That's pretty much why I left."

"Were they sinking fast, and you jumped off before the ship went under, or what?" Jerry probed.

"No, they weren't sinking, and they aren't today. They are a strong competitor. I had some deep roots there, and some very strong associations. I lost a very close friend that I worked with there. It was a tragedy and maybe we'll talk about it later, but for now, it's in the past."

The tone of Les's voice told Jerry that the story of Les Brigham and Morphics was not up for discussion on this trip.

"Jerry, we have some great customers to see on this trip, and I think you will really enjoy the experience."

Traffic was light this morning. Not much of a line up at the metered freeway onramp.

"This is a good sign Jerry. Light traffic. Usually means a productive and profitable trip."

"Hey Jerry, let's start this trip off as planned. Did you get a chance to give any thoughts to those questions I asked you?"

"Absolutely!" Jerry responded exuberantly. "Where do you want to begin?"

As Jerry is responding to Les's question he reaches down on the floor and pulls out his notebook. By all indications it is looking like Jerry has given a lot of thought about this trip, and has compiled quite an agenda of questions.

"Are those all questions?" Les asks Jerry after glancing at his notebook.

"Absolutely. I have a ton of them and hopefully we can talk about them all. This isn't going to be a 'hobby' for me." Jerry grins.

Inside, Les Brigham is ecstatic. He's got a person in the car that is interested in what he has done all of his life. Les feels that his experience is going to be interpreted as valuable. This kind of situation doesn't come along every day for him.

"OK, let's cover my first requests, and then we can start on your list."

"Let's start with why you pursued this particular position, and what do you want to accomplish on the big scale?"

Jerry inhaled deep and repositioned himself in the seat of the car. He shuffled some papers and convinced Les that he had given the questions some valuable thought.

"Well, first of all I want to earn a decent income. That's probably the number one goal."

Les nodded.

"Then I want to become an expert in my chosen field, although I suppose that was a given."

"Great! I know I didn't ask you this, but what is going to be your campaign slogan?"

"My what," Jerry asked surprised.

"Let me re-word it. What traits are you going to develop to earn that income as well as become the expert?"

"I'm assuming that if I know enough about what I do, people will sense that from me, and want to have me help them. I can help by selling them products. The more they buy the more income I produce. So, learning will be my first objective. That's the condensed version Les. How does that sound?"

"You are on the right track." Les responds.

"You have a beginning and an end. We can call it a preconceived plan. Now early on let's define it in detail, and draw the picture that you can clearly identify with. That picture needs to be perfectly clear and concise. Then all you have to do is live it."

"Are you going to help me draw that picture Les?" Jerry asks optimistically.

"I am, if you want me to. We can probably work on it together when you start to develop your territory."

Again, Les knew his future and realized that he probably wouldn't be there the whole time of Jerry's initial growing period. But Les also knew that plans can change, so he felt that he wasn't really misleading Jerry.

"Absolutely! Let's make sure we use colored pencils."

"It's the only ones I use." Les responds.

"OK, the second part of your assignment was to identify people in your life that shared this occupation. I wanted to know what you thought of them. I think that is what I asked, wasn't it?"

"Les, I don't know anyone in the industrial supply business. I know some guys that are territory managers and that have geographical territories. They travel quite a bit. I thought about my responses based on my knowledge of them. Is that OK?"

"Absolutely dude, I just wanted you to reflect on someone that you can identify with and share your opinion. One of those guys will be perfect."

"So pick one of the guys and tell me about him." Les continues.

"Perfect. Let me tell you about Byron Maxwell. He's my neighbor."

"Byron works as a salesperson for a mattress manufacturer. He has been there quite a while. I believe the company is headquartered in the south. He is gone most of the week and normally home on weekends."

"Do you know him well or talk to him much?" Les inquires.

"I have had some conversations with Byron. He paints a fairly positive picture of what he does. He seems to enjoy it."

"Tell me more about Byron. What kind of guy is he? Do you trust him? How does he represent himself?" Les pushes.

"I know he is single, about my age, mid 30's. Seems to know some wealthy folks, judging by the cars I see at his house sometimes. I think he drinks his share. His face is red and blotchy. He seems to be a heck of a nice guy. Probably finds it difficult to push himself away from the dinner table as well. He appears a bit overweight. I've watched him start and stop an exercise routine many times. He goes out and buys real fancy sweat suits and running shoes. Then I see him exercise a couple of times and then nothing."

"OK."

"He also wears a lot of jewelry and bling. Sometimes I see him sparkle in the distance before I can make out who he is."

Les smirks at Jerry's comment. "That's funny."

"Would you place Byron as a role model for anyone, relating to his occupation?"

"I'm not sure. Like I said before, he seems to be a nice guy but in some ways he's a bit creepy."

"Creepy how?" Les questions.

"Well, I don't have anything against a guy the wears flashy jewelry. That's a matter of what a person likes. I'm sure folks wear jewelry for confidence reasons as well as to enhance their image of success. I guess the big deal for me is how he takes care of himself. I have a tough time integrating the image of a successful person with someone that has let themselves go physically as well as looks a little sloppy. That's probably it exactly."

"Jerry, I agree one hundred percent. However, I know a lot of fairly sloppy individuals that are stellar salespeople as well as great individuals. But you're correct. A sloppy surface appearance puts up a small wall right from the start."

"We as professionals need to stay healthy. We need to control our diet, and exercise. It is imperative. It is vital. A healthy routine alone will produce energy for you. It will even knock out the attitude slumps, and take away many of the unnecessary worries. It will detour you from over thinking and dwelling on the wrong things. Dude, it is absolutely vital!"

"We have to also realize that just eating right and exercising won't turn us into successful salespeople, but it will open up, and keep those doors open for our success to wander in."

Les felt that he needed to add one more thought. He is so driven about this type of topic it's really hard for him to stop.

"The travelling routine can be hell on your eating impulses. So many times my meals get neglected because of priorities and commitments that I have made. I get so damn hungry that the best thing to eat is whatever is fast and filling. It's at that point that my body is low on calories, my brain is misfiring and I enjoy a quick, unhealthy meal to be followed by a long session of self guilt. It's not a positive routine."

Jerry looks concerned. "So, what do you do?"

"You make a conscious effort to eat at correct intervals. And, you learn what can be eaten and where to get the best food. A lot of fast food places make some pretty awesome salads. And when you are hungry enough, they taste real good!"

"Wow Les, I honestly didn't think I was going to get trained on eating as well. I was just kidding about my comment a few weeks ago about stopping the sweets and help me lose weight."

"Well just think. You already got more than you expected then."

"OK, enough about eating. Let's talk about selling and this crazy occupation." Les says.

"Jerry, explain to me in very few words, how 'selling' is defined in your mind."

"In general Les, it's probably about getting people to buy what you are representing. Wouldn't you say?"

"Yeah, probably. That is what the end result must be or else you will have a short career. Do you mind if I break this down to the basics? At least in my mind what I think it is."

"Sure, I'd love to hear it. Lay it on me."

"I guess the question is then, what do you need to do to be successful in selling? It's a big question in my opinion. You will also get a myriad of answers to that question depending on who you ask."

"And by the way. Just because you are riding with me this week, and I'm spouting off about my way of doing things, doesn't mean that they are correct for you. My thoughts and principles work for me. I can do this job with these beliefs. I'm sure some would also disagree with a few of my thoughts."

"I'm cool with that Les. It should make for great discussion. I'm listening anyway."

"OK, Jerry. Thanks."

"Here are the key points, or the starter package to success in a sales occupation. And again, remember this is an opinion only."

"Sure," Jerry responds.

Les holds up fingers as to count as he is reciting the answers to the question.

"Number one. You need enthusiasm with tenacity."

"Number two. Organizational skills."

"Number three. Product knowledge."

"Number four. Intelligence with common sense."

"Number five. Honesty."

"Number six. Integrity." He holds onto the steering wheel while raising up his index finger."

"I feel that when you find an individual with those traits, there's a strong chance you'll produce a very successful result."

"So, those traits help us sell more?" Jerry inquires.

Les responds with more questions, followed by short, to the point answers.

"Well, first of all is this career all about selling? Maybe."

"Is it all about just talking about your product? No, probably not."

"Is it all about closing the sale? Closing is very important and some type of a purchasing agreement must be agreed upon to actually consider it a sale."

"Is it all about making money and commissions? Maybe. This depends on what your motivating factor is and money is a big one."

"I never thought about it like this before Les." Jerry says.

"I know Jerry, few take the time, or even feel that they have the time to analyze the process like this."

Les continues.

"Let's look at this 'selling' concept and our role in its simplest form."

"Companies produce a product, or offer a service to other individuals or organizations for exchange of money."

"So far so good," Les inquires.

Jerry nods affirmative.

"This offer, that the product or service is available, needs to be announced or publicized."

"Some of those products or services need explaining with more detail in order for the benefit to be realized. A human interface is perceived to be required to complete the acceptance and implementation process."

"In other words, sales representatives are needed to do some in depth explaining and provide help in the acceptance and implementation process." Jerry chimes in.

"Exactly. We help the prospective customer make intelligent decisions."

"In exchange for creating the successful implementation of that product or service to another individual or organization, the sales representative receives a monetary reward. It's called a commission."

"That's the first description. Now in a less lengthy fashion, OK?"

Jerry seems quite interested.

"A company has something that they want to sell, and they feel that they need a sales representative to provide the help to get that accomplished from introduction to receipt of money. A sales representative gets paid for creating that success."

"Does any of that make sense Jerry, or did I get off on a ramble?"

"I think it makes a lot of sense Les. I actually understand your viewpoint. But, it sure opens up the door for a lot of questions."

"Ask away, we are in this car for the next few days between calls. Besides I love to talk about this as you can probably tell."

"Oh yeah, I can tell. It seems like there are a lot of things to think about. I thought I could just go out and talk, and people would buy. Now I'm not so sure I had it figured out. It seems stressful."

"It's really not stressful Jerry, if you stay on focus. But, it can get stressful. We are dealing with a range of personalities, and that can be a challenge in itself."

"Do you think the stress will affect me as well Les?"

"It sure can if you let it."

"This will probably be your biggest challenge. Stress is always a challenge, and is no stranger in the selling world. Try to find ways to keep stress to a minimum. It is impossible to be in control of every situation, but it is possible much of the time to be in control of your own actions and reactions."

"And how do I do that?" Jerry asks.

"Determine early what types of things push your buttons."

"Don't avoid situations that can stress you, but have a solid grounding understanding of what is trying to take place. For instance, if you get into a situation with a customer and the customer seems unreasonable. It is imperative that you look at the situation from the customer's viewpoint. And sometimes you have to look fairly deep."

"Many times our customers may not have thought through what they are saying, and are just acting out. Remember, in their mind many times, you are there only trying to sell them something, or resolve an issue that they have been struggling with. In their mind they owe you nothing. They just want it fixed, and it is your job to fix it. Let's reword that. It is mainly your opportunity."

"Also, don't look to your customer for strength and reassurance, especially in the beginning of a sales relationship. Chances are, they may not be easy on you."

"I'm sure of that," Jerry responds.

"You know, I often think that people who enjoy puzzles would make very good salespeople. If you think about it from an over simplified viewpoint, solving puzzles is creating solutions. Puzzle masters enjoy the search for the 'fix.' They thrive on the challenge. It is not stress for them."

"I never thought of it that way Les, but you are right. We're just looking for solutions."

"Exactly!"

"You really get 'wound up' on this helping theory, don't you Les? And honestly, I don't mean that in a bad way."

"Sure, I understand. It's a philosophy that I almost worship, to create the magic that usually takes place."

"Just to make this point even stronger, let's look at it again from this viewpoint."

"As we break the 'selling as helping' concept down, it really boils down mostly to helping. This is important. I think it should be our grounding force."

"Think about this primitive analogy. Needing something is within all of us. We all need something, 24 hours a day, seven days a week. This happens in our personal life as well as our professional world. If we resolve that need, that particular need is no longer existent."

"What does this have to do with selling?" Jerry asks puzzled.

"It depends."

"If you paid something for the resolve, you bought it. And yes, someone sold it to you. Even if it was a cashier at a grocery store, they received your money, in exchange for their resolve."

"Salespeople are individuals that are armed daily with helping solutions for select people or companies. Their job is to find those in need of their solutions. It's that simple. If no one needed anything, salespeople would be out of a job. It is imperative that you keep the helping concept in your mind always."

"I'm getting it I think." Jerry responds.

"You could also interpret our roles as we are individuals that find ways to create needs. And quite honestly, that's not far off either."

"That would be compared to saying that 'I didn't realize how hungry I was until I saw that juicy hamburger on TV." Jerry tosses out.

"That fits as well." Les agrees.

"So, do we focus less on closing sales, and more on helping?"

"Well, if we help enough, we should close enough sales. Zig Ziglar states, "You will get what you want, when you help enough people get what they want.""

"Closing a sale is merely nothing more than creating an agreement to purchase. And in even simpler terms, it's getting an approval and exchange of money for products, or services offered."

"Then why do some individuals put a negative spin on salespeople? All they are really doing is helping."

"Probably the frustration comes when the focus is put on using manipulative diversion techniques to change the mindset of the customer. During the mindset change, the salesperson has the customer agree to buy. The result can be an unhappy customer."

"It's really about ethics and character then isn't it?" Jerry asks innocently.

"A lot of it yes. I could also attempt to add that real professional salespeople don't have to intentionally close a sale, but that would be a fallacy. Some customers do need the help, or the nudge to make a positive decision. I feel that if we have the solution for them, and it is the best solution for them, we owe it to them to be sure there are no doubts as to why we should be the ones to help them. However in doing this, we do not need to be overly aggressive or deceptive. We can however be assertive, and consistent and honest. There is a big difference between aggressive and assertive."

"Do you mean assertive, as in keep asking for the business?" Jerry inquires.

"As professional salespeople we change colors many times. It's not so much asking consistently for a 'yes,' as though we must listen and suggest constantly."

"We as professionals must be consistently aware of the customer's emotions, and their body language. This tells us how receptive they are to our solution offering. We must style flex as well to make sure they know we are there to help them."

"So, if they run from us do we chase them?" Jerry asks in a semi joking way.

"It totally depends on how we chase. It also depends on how strongly we feel about our solution."

"I really didn't think that there was this much to the process. I thought I would just keep seeing folks until they bought something from me. I may have been wrong."

"You aren't wrong Jerry, we just haven't discussed one important concept."

"What's that?"

"Trust. It's a big deal, and it just may be the 'whole deal.'"

"Gaining trust in a customer is another pinnacle point in building a relationship. As I said, it could be the most important one. The 'rock solid' key to gaining trust with a customer is that the process can not be faked. And I don't say that as don't fake it, you just can't fake it. It will not happen. If by some miracle you do gain trust with a customer by faking it, your customer is a short term affair. This customer will fall for the next imposter that comes around, and you will be out of their life."

"Here's an analogy. Try this one OK?" Les asks.

"I will admit something. I am a great swimmer! As long as the water is not over my head. I can't swim in 8 foot water. I am only 6' 4" tall. If I was interested in learning to be a confident swimmer, I would probably need someone to teach me."

"OK, so…"

"Let me re-phrase that. I would probably need to find someone that had the skills to teach me, that I could exchange money for their service. Currently I don't have the desire to become a confident swimmer. When I do there are plenty of individuals out there that have that skill in their solutions kit."

"How important do you think trust will be with me when I get in the water with them?"

"I get your point Les, loud and clear."

"Just for the sake of talking, Jerry are you a good swimmer?"

"Yes, as a matter of fact I am, but I still get the point."

"Cool, if this little swimming analogy doesn't work for you try skydiving with a teacher you don't trust."

They both laughed.

"Les, I realize what happens if I really don't have a sincere interest in the customer. And we can even take it a step further and say if I have no sincere interest in any customers. I just lose. It's simple. I just lose."

"You got it, I had no doubt!" Les smiles.

"You know Jerry, you will find tons of prospective customers that you will try and get to know. Some successful, and others not so much."

"I know."

"Personalities are as numerous as the stars. Everyone is different. My personal theory is that I will sell much less to people that I struggle in communication with, than those that I get along with. And by the way, it's not my personal theory it's just plain human nature."

The two men had been driving now for about two hours.

"Would you mind pulling into the next available Rest Area? I need to get out and stretch my legs." Jerry asked.

"No problem rookie, getting a little cramped up?"

"Yeah, and I need to make a phone call." Les adds.

"I reduced drinking coffee just for that reason."

"There is a place to stop about 10 miles farther. It's a little convenience store and gas station. They have awesome sweet rolls. Every so often I indulge. I'll get us a couple. It will be my treat."

Jerry laughs. "Now I'm living the dream Mr. Brigham."

"It just gets better from here. But it kind of devalues the earlier conversation about eating healthy." Les responds.

Jerry laughs.

Les turns off the freeway and the two men arrive at the little store. The rest rooms are on the outside of the building. Jerry heads over to the men's room and Les goes inside to greet the owners.

"You got your boss with you today Les? Rudy the store owner asks.

"No Rudy, just a new guy. They're sending him out with me to see if I can talk him out of committing his life to the 'asphalt ribbon.'"

"Where's Luna?"

Luna is Rudy's wife. She makes the sweet rolls that bring people in from all over.

"She's visiting the daughter over in Poldville. We just had our first grandchild."

"Congratulations Rudy, I am very happy for you two. But, don't you think you two are a little young to be grandparents?"

"Heck yes, but that's what you get for falling in love with your high school sweetheart, and starting a family early."

"I totally understand, remember, I married mine as well."

"By the way, where are those great sweet rolls? I got Jerry all jacked up about how delicious they are, and I am starting to panic. I don't see them."

"As you know Les, Luna's the baker in the family. We'll have them back in the case later this week."

"Great, I think we are coming back this way, we'll be sure and swing by."

Jerry comes in through the front door.

"By the way, Rudy, this is Jerry Feldman. He's my student for the week. Just think how I get to pollute his brain with all my pathetic beliefs."

"You're in for it kid, Rudy says to Jerry. But don't let this guy fool you. He is a true and genuine good guy. He'll take good care of you."

"I'm sure of it," Jerry responds. "I'm not worried at all."

Rudy and Jerry exchange conversation while Les excuses himself to use the restroom.

Les goes back in the store to get Jerry and they head back out to the car. Les turns back one more time.

"Congratulations again Rudy, give them all hugs for me."

"I sure will Les, take care of the new guy. And stop back through if you get the chance. Luna will be sorry she missed you."

"Take care buddy."

As they approach Les's car Les asks Jerry to wait for him while he makes a quick call on his cell phone. He needs to check in with Cindy to see if she was able to arrange a time for them to meet with the attorney regarding the transaction with the Winman's.

It was a very amiable arrangement with the Winman's. Frank and Sarah had nothing but great intentions for the Brigham's by taking over Layman and Son's.

As explained by Frank and Sarah Winman to the Brigham's initially this would be a win-win arrangement for both parties. Frank and Sarah were getting out of the business and starting a fantasy life. Les and Cindy were taking over an extremely lucrative business and building their own fortune. The Winman's were extremely sensitive to the concerns of the Brigham's and trusted that all would work out.

"Were you able to get an appointment with Chausler and Bach?" Les asked Cindy, without even saying hello.

"Well hi honey, how are you?" Cindy responded in a sarcastic tone.

"Cin, I'm sorry, my mind is going ninety miles and hour this morning and I've got the new guy with me. I'm trying to compartmentalize all my thoughts and concerns so Jerry get's some good out of the trip, yet I'm totally engrossed in this decision of ours. It is giving me a headache."

"Don't worry, I realize what is happening." Cindy replies sympathetically. "My mind is all over the place as well."

"Do you think we are doing the right thing Les?" Cindy asks with an all but confident tone.

"I sure hope so sweetie. We have both seen what the business is and we both know that we can manage it." Les responds.

"I think that we are fools not to move on this." Les continues.

"I know. I keep thinking the same thing as well."

"We're not all that old either Cindy. I'm really not worried about the age aspect even though I may say I am at times. I was always thinking about starting a business of my own when I retired anyway. This way we'll be way ahead of the game."

"I hope so Les, I sure hope so."

"I arranged an appointment with them Thursday afternoon. I was going to call you but you said that you would call me when you got the chance." Cindy states.

"No problem sweetie. I just can't share any of this with the new hired guy. I really don't know him, and it would deflate any impact the trip may have if he knew I was on my way out."

Just hearing those words come out of his mouth gave Les a strange feeling. He had worked for someone else his whole life and really never truly imagined himself running his own company. There were certainly doubts.

"I got to go. I'll call you tonight babe." Les hangs up.

Chapter Two

CHAPTER THREE

The day was turning out to be absolutely gorgeous. The spring temperature was still a bit brisk, but the budding trees along the route made it a wonderful sight.

"Rudy seems to be a nice guy. How long have you known him?"

"Not a long time. About three years at most."

"He sure seems to think a lot of you. Like everyone I have met, I may add." Jerry states confidently.

"I just get to know folks because I see them frequently. I also like to ask questions, because I want to know more about them. It's almost like an obsession. I'm just curious. Mostly because I want to find out if we know anyone in common. It's amazing how many folks have some common thread, but we have to ask a few questions to find out that information."

"Isn't it kind of prying into their affairs?" Jerry asks.

"Not even close. Most folks usually find it nice and flattering to have someone show interest in them. Remember when it comes to discussions, and an especially sales discussion, everyone's favorite radio station is WII-FM.

"WII-FM, let's see what does that stand for.....I could guess, but I'll let you tell me."

"It stands for 'What's In It For Me.' Everyone's favorite topic of conversation is themselves. We all like to be asked about ourselves and hear our own name being spoken. It is just common human communication."

"I guess you're right. It's fun having someone act interested in me, or about who I am. It's flattering."

"It's one of the easiest things you can do Jerry to get to know people. Treat them like they are the most important person in the world, because deep down, in their mind, they are. It absolutely works magic."

"I hate to burst your bubble Les, but I know people that don't like talking about themselves. I have friends like that."

"Sure you do Jerry, so do I. However, if I started to talk to one of your friends and ask them questions, they probably wouldn't be offended, if the conversation flowed innocently. I could probably find out plenty about one of 'those' friends, as you could with some of mine as well."

"You're probably right. Les."

"Dude, it's like making sales calls without appointments. A lot of these people will shut you out immediately because they just don't have an interest in what you are offering. Their mind isn't ready to let you in. They could probably use what you are offering, but it isn't that important to them at that particular moment. Here's an example."

"OK."

"How would you feel if one day your door bell rang?"

"You were busy on a very important project. The project had a deadline that you had to meet. When you answered the door, a person at the other end just started to talk to you about something that your didn't care about. They wouldn't shut up, and just kept talking. They even squeezed their way into your home as well, so now they are inside your own personal space."

"Still with me Jerry?"

"Oh yeah, keep going."

"If this scenario actually took place would it even matter what they were talking about? Feeling like you are imposed upon is not a comforting feeling. No one likes being imposed upon."

"Do you agree with that?"

"I sure do, I hate it."

"Now let's change the atmosphere."

"Same person, same day. For the prior two weeks, you have been thinking about having your house pressure washed. When the doorbell rings the person outside introduces them self and quickly hands you a flyer about home pressure washing."

Les looks at Jerry.

"Would you invite him in?"

"It depends." Jerry replied.

"Sure, it probably depends on many things, but one thing is certain. You would be interested in what he has to say. If you didn't interview him at that instant, you probably would call him later to find out more about his offerings."

"The point is, everyone is busy. We protect our time by quickly qualifying how a particular type of input will benefit us."

"So then are you saying Les, the key to success on getting someone's attention is by creating a unique approach? If that is the case, I could dress up in a chicken outfit and be unique. I could walk in the door cackling. I'm sure that they would probably remember me for some time."

"You know Jerry, in many types of sales jobs it could be a great idea. However in our industry, we try hard to be knowledgeable individuals. There's something about a chicken outfit that contradicts that image."

Les keeps talking.

"Try to be unique. Every one of us are unique. We look different. We act different. We talk different. But in the eyes of a stranger, we may just blend in unnoticeably with the rest of society."

"We can be unique in a myriad of ways. Think of your particular industry, and evaluate those individuals out in the world doing the same thing you are."

"Do you mean my competitors?" Jerry asks.

"Exactly, do you know how they project themselves? Do you know how they act? Probably not. I will bet though, that you have heard about the slightly less than honest ones. I'll bet you have heard about the pushy ones. Even those that are less than knowledgeable. Could you capitalize on that?"

"As we just touched on a minute ago, the foremost method that comes to mind is to be the most knowledgeable. It is however the toughest one. Especially if you are new to your profession."

"But it may always be your driving force in this profession. It is also the easiest way of gaining trust with a customer if used correctly."

"Another Cardinal Rule, and something worth mentioning in respect to knowledge. We as salespeople hate being asked a question that we don't have an answer for. Many salespeople have that as their number one fear. They dread the thought. It may purely be an ego thing."

"Don't ever answer questions inaccurate, just to answer questions."

"Why?" Jerry asks innocently but with a comical look in his eye.

"You're messing with me now dude. But merely to torture you I'm going to answer."

"I think it is like juggling razor sharp swords. The professional jugglers that do that sort of thing know how to do it. They never sweat. All it takes is one slip, or one incorrectly answered question, and your game is stacked against you. Your credibility is now in question."

"Are you saying that only professional salespeople can falsely answer questions, when they don't know the answers?"

"No, not at all. Professional salespeople just don't do it. Building that credibility and trust is such an important thing to build, any intelligent, professional will not jeopardize it."

"I totally understand Les. This totally applies to the part about being unique as well. All we have is ourselves. I'm sure that in this industry our competitors have the same literature, the same type of products, the same issues with their shipping department, and the same personality issues with their customer service representatives."

"Exactly. The only thing that we have to sell is ourselves. Our own internal personality and ethics as to how we do our job. And I might add we hope that our customer sees that in us and values it as well."

"Yep, even the toughest prospect in the world. They may look uninterested and uninvolved. However they record in their minds how you conducted yourself with them. They can't and won't erase it."

"Does this kind of talk make you nervous?" Les asks.

"It sure could, Jerry says, but, only if I am pretending to be someone that I am not."

"Right on! Confidence and peace in this profession come from being genuine. Nervousness will go away as you gain more experience. The experience will give you knowledge, and the two of them will give you confidence."

"You know Jerry, we make a lot of friends in this business. But in spite of what we may think, only a very small group of these 'friends' care as much about us as we care about them."

"Now, that's just my opinion, but it's not far off."

"The friendship thing works well from both sides. We like creating the friendships because it gives us a sense of accomplishment, as well as a warm fuzzy feeling knowing we have earned a perceived loyal customer. And as a bonus a new friend."

"I sense a 'but' coming." Jerry inquires.

"You're right. Many of those customers care much more about what you can, and will do for them, rather than wallowing in the experience of the friendship. Wait until a problem comes up. That friendship could be tested. Especially if you have to support one of your company's policies, and it differs from your customer's opinion."

"So, are you saying that our friendships with our customers are phony?"

"No, not at all, but most of them may be a bit different than other personal friendships."

"I can sure see how a person could get involved with helping a customer. Especially if it is driven from a true helping viewpoint. It could lead one to believe they have secured loyal friends."

"I totally agree."

"Just stay focused, and keep it real. You'll receive plenty of rewards."

Les and Jerry were getting close to their first stop on the trip.

CHAPTER FOUR

"Jerry, this is our first stop. We're going in here to see Max Cline. He's the Purchasing Agent for this operation. Quite honestly, he's really a fairly nice guy, but he gets his kicks out of trying to compare my prices to everyone else. He is always squawking about how high our prices are and buys small amounts. He also keeps using 'company policy' as an excuse. He spends hours every week looking for the cheapest material, and messes up their production when the crap they end up buying falls short of their expectations."

"Does he tell you those things?" Jerry asks.

"Not directly, but I read between the lines during conversations."

"Watch how this goes. I like to have fun with him whenever I can. It makes it worth stopping by."

"What are you going to do Les, slap him around stick his head in the toilet?"

"Heck no. Not to that extreme. Just watch."

"If he buys little from you, why do you see him at all?"

"That's a good question Jerry, and I'm glad you asked. Triton Manufacturing here is a very small player based on individual purchases. However, they are owned by a much larger operation in the Northeast, and I'm thinking someday things may change. You never know who you are talking to either. This guy could someday end up working for another company that has different policies, or they could be bought out and change their purchasing habits. And last but not least, this guy could leave and be replaced by someone else. I want my books all over the place if a new guy comes to town. Does it make sense?"

"Sure." Jerry responds.

The two men walk in the door and head back to Max's office. The door is open so they walk in.

Max Cline is a little man with a "clown cut" hairstyle. He looks up from his desk.

"Mr. Brigham, what brings you to this lonely part of the country?"

"Hey Max, how are you? We're just out seeing my favorite and highest revenue producing customers."

Max laughs.

"I didn't know I was one of your favorites, because I know for damn sure we're not one of your highest revenue producers. If we are, I need to send flowers to your company as a sympathy gesture."

"I couldn't resist. I had to say that."

"I know, I know." Max responds.

"Max, this is Jerry Feldman. He's a new employee, and he is riding with me for a few days to get a feel for the business. So be nice to him. And as long as I am at it, be nice to me for a change and give me a big order for something." Les is smiling.

Max grins.

"Les, I have told you many, many times. Your prices are too high. I buy what I can from you, but I get hammered if my production costs go out of line."

"Max, that is the same old line you have been using on me since we met. I think it's time you changed to another excuse. Would you like me to counter that objection?"

"Sure. Go ahead Les. You're going to anyway."

"Max, remember the last time I was in here with a special on those Embossed Ratchet Hubs? You said that someone had a better price and you had to get the lowest quote? Do you remember that Max?"

Les was smiling as he was talking, so it wasn't a lecture or an interrogation. Besides he knew Max could go weird on him in a moments notice. He had seen it before.

Les also knew that he had to teach something to Jerry on this visit as well. If all went well, this visit would give the two men more to talk about on their next segment of travel.

"How prompt did the order get delivered? What was the quality like? And one more question. What was the total invoice amount including shipping and packing?"

Max looked down for a minute stalling for answers.

"Les, I'll be glad to answer the questions. And because I actually do have respect for you I will answer candidly."

"In hindsight I probably should have taken your quote. The supplier lagged on the delivery, but we were able to get the production run accomplished on time."

"As for the quality, I'm pretty sure it was the same exact item. It would have been a 'buy out' for you as well. I know ContainPro doesn't make them."

"This time they added a fairly hefty freight charge on the invoice. Final total would have equaled your quote."

"Max, do you think we would have delivered on time?" Les asks.

"As a matter of fact, Les, I think you would have. Damn it man, why do you always have to catch me when I made a questionable decision?" Max chuckles as he makes the statement.

"I wasn't trying to catch you at all dude, I just am very connected to who my competitors are, and how they sell and deliver their products and services. My fantasy is that someday I will walk in here and you will say to me that your organization has decided to base their purchasing habits on total results and profitability of the vendor. It's at that exact time I will realize that I have done my job and have been providing the correct message to you."

Max looks at Les in an odd way and then at Jerry. He then picks up the phone.

"Lou, it's Max. Would you come in to my office for a minute. I've got Les Brigham from ContainPro in here. Thanks."

"Whoa man!" Les gasps.

"Are you calling in some backup?"

"Relax, I just want you to hear something. You may be shocked, so remain seated."

An older gentleman with silver hair walks in. Les has met him before.

"Lou Riley, you remember Les Brigham. This is one of Les's new trainees. Jerry… was it?"

"Yes sir, Jerry Feldman. Pleased to meet you Mr. Riley."

"Same here," addressing Jerry then he turns to Les.

"Mr. Brigham, how have you been?"

"Just great Lou, trying to convince Max that ContainPro can do a lot for you guys. I'm just continuing to scratch at the door."

Lou Riley is the Vice President of Triton Manufacturing.

Max directs his attention to Lou.

"Lou, I'm not putting you on the spot because you and I have talked about this before. I just want Les to hear about the concept that you and I have been talking about. You know what I am talking about right?"

"Sure, about the 'vendor value program' that we have been trying to implement?" Lou responds.

"Exactly."

"Les, here is the thing. We are realizing the market is changing. The young and growing companies are making purchasing decisions based on price alone. It's the Millennium generation. Tech and information based decisions. We are not like that and need to look at a more grass roots method of looking at production costs."

Les is listening intently, and Jerry is trying to guess where this is going.

"I am going to give you an opportunity." Max states.

"Within the next 30 days I want you to interview for a position in our company."

Les looks puzzled, and poor Jerry is really twisted up. "Are they trying to hire Les?" is his first thought.

Les has been around, and is putting the comments into perspective. He thinks he knows where Max is going.

"Les, I'm buying material from a host of vendors with no consistency. We're starting to think about the bottom line value of a supplier as a business partner. We have built no real loyalty to anyone, and for a long time it has seemed like the best way to run our organization. Lou and I have decided to look at a different approach."

"I think I'm following along." Les interjects.

"Les, would you put together a pseudo proposal as to how you can help us trim our costs by providing a more comprehensive menu of your company's services and products. I'll give you any information you need to provide us with accurate feedback."

Les is sitting still, fingers interlaced and listening intently. Jerry interprets this as a marriage proposal.

Lou Riley is watching both Les and Jerry at this point to see if this has raised their interest. Lou is hoping that Les gets giddy at the opportunity and is anticipating that reaction.

Les stays calm for an instant. He then raises one eyebrow and asks.

"Am I, or rather will I be the only vendor providing this type of information?"

Lou and Max both glance over at each other. Max looks down at his desk.

"No, actually Les, we are asking all of our vendors for this type of information. Our goal is to have a preferred vendor chosen by the end of next quarter."

Jerry's face drops and he looks like he just got kicked in the gut. He was anticipating that Les was going to be the "Prom Queen" for this company, and now he realizes that he's just going to be in a pack of contenders vying for an offer.

"I will be happy to provide you with a comprehensive proposal based on information that I receive from you. How soon could you spend a couple of hours with me to tour the facility, followed up by a meeting to explain in depth, your new business focus?"

Lou and Max both perk up at that point. Most vendors have just wanted a list of goods to quote on. They then throw in a bunch of promises on a cover letter and mail it back. The vendor then follows up by a bunch of annoying phone calls asking for the key to the "front gate."

"Les, I could do this at most anytime convenient for you. Just name a date."

"Max, I have this week full already, and want to be sure Jerry gets his money's worth from me."

Les has his calendar on his lap opened up and ready.

"I could meet with you in two weeks from this day. After our meeting I will need three weeks to provide the information that you are requesting. Now that is outside of your 30 day timeframe that you requested, but I'm not going to just throw you some prices and hope we are lowest bid. I believe you are looking for a more comprehensive vendor relationship, and quite honestly that is what I look for on a daily basis."

Les continues. "I'll tell you right now, ContainPro will not be the cheapest player in this contest. We aren't in the discount business. We provide a total Return on Investment approach to our more valued customers. Our policies, backed up by our customer service should by far outweigh any cost objection. And, by the way it is my responsibility to explain that theory and explain to you as to why I can say it with confidence."

Lou Riley responds.

"Les, I think that your proposal will be the one we will anticipate the most. Thank you for your interest."

Lou stands up and shakes Les's hand. And then to Jerry.

"Thank you for your interest Lou." Les responds.

"Learn what you can from this guy." Lou says to Jerry. "I think you got lucky to work with him."

Les smiles. "Thanks Lou. That's nice of you to say."

Lou Riley heads back to his office. As Les and Jerry say their goodbye's to Max, Les asks Max a question.

"Max, just a question."

"What?"

"Are you folks still buying 4 inch spindle adapters?"

"Oh yeah, cases of them. I get them cheap brought in from Mexico."

"Aluminum, or an alloy?" Les knew the answer, but he wanted to hear Max answer.

"Aluminum, they are the least expensive. Why?"

"Would you agree that they are a disposable item for you?"

"Disposable, as in using them up in our machining process, yes. They get destroyed daily by the milling machines."

Les asks another question that he already knows the answer to.

"What wears out? Do you know?"

"Sure, the center hole starts to wear and then it causes havoc on the rest of the machining process."

"How many do you usually buy? Actually let me rephrase that. How many do you go through in a year?" Les is holding a profitable solution for Max and is about to lay it right on his lap."

"Maybe 1500 a year. But I get them cheap remember/"

"We are just releasing that same product with a bronze bushing inside. They will last 10 times longer and the price is reasonable."

"How reasonable?" Max has to ask.

"About three times more than you are paying now for your import piece."

"How much longer will they last again?" Max asks.

"Studies show a minimum of ten times the life span of a domestic aluminum spindle. Could be increased considering an inexpensive imported piece."

"Any samples with you today?"

"No. And I wouldn't sample them if I had to."

"Why?"

"Because they come with a guarantee. We branded them with a guarantee to outlast any competitive product. Give me a PO for a case of them and try them out. It will be the best thing you do today. No joking."

"What if I win the lottery? These stupid adapters won't even exist if that happens."

"I meant within reason of course." Les adds. They all laugh.

Max goes to his keyboard and creates a Purchase Order to ContainPro for a case of adapters.

"I trust you Les. Don't worry."

"I'm not worried at all. I'm glad you're starting to make good decisions." Les throws out with a big grin and then extends his hand for a shake.

As they get into the car Les puts his hand on Jerry's shoulder and says, "I bet you think that was a roller coaster ride worth remembering?"

"As a matter of fact, yes. That's exactly what I thought it was. At first I thought they were going to gang up on you about some pricing structure, and then I thought that they were offering you some type of special opportunity. Something makes me think you walked out of there better off."

"Absolutely we did. We accomplished exactly what I try to get done with most every customer."

"What's that Les, besides getting orders?"

"I strive for that chance to go above and beyond the expected. I could have just pushed for a bid list and walked out. That's what every rookie salesperson would do. Given the history and the attitude of that company, almost any representative would have done just that."

"Why didn't you then? You were implying that they are just cost conscious buyers, and you like to have fun just pushing Max's buttons. I didn't see any 'button pushing' in there, just a response to do what they asked."

"It was a break that comes along much too seldom. Purchasing guys like Max get into ruts and routines. They hear the same old thing day in and day out from suppliers. The new guys are trained to just go in and get the orders. Keep pushing for the order. Close the deal, etcetera, etcetera, etcetera."

"And…" Jerry asks.

"It's a routine that really never helps develop any type of lasting relationship, or even a valuable customer relationship. It's what creates the attitudes of purchasing people like Max Cline. No one ever gets the chance to perform the value added service that separates the quality salespeople and suppliers from all the rest."

Les continues. "The first thing that I needed to establish is if this was just an act. Sometimes purchasing guys will throw out a block like this request. Wanting someone to spend a little time and effort can sometime be just a test to see if they have a hard working conscientious sales representative. It's how some of these dudes 'cull the herd' so to speak."

"I can see that." Jerry says.

"I refuse to let opportunities like this go unanswered. Even if it is possibly just a hoop they want me to jump through."

"But here is the thing. I'm going to blow these folks away with attention and effort. They do enough volume with my competition it could produce a very nice account for ContainPro if they start to show any type of loyalty. And that is what I am trying to earn from them, loyalty. I have this opportunity and I will not let it go unanswered."

"One more thing." Les holds his hand up.

"What?" Jerry asks.

"Did you notice that at the end when I asked for the PO for the adapters Max turned around and printed a PO?"

"So," Jerry remarks.

"That wouldn't have happened in that office normally. We had established the feeling that we had value. They are now anticipating our proposal, and feel that they will be helped. When I asked for an order for those adapters, even though they are more expensive, I got little resistance."

"But they are better than they are using now, and they have a guarantee. Anybody would have bought them. Wouldn't they have?"

"Not Max Cline, I can tell you that."

Les felt he needed to be sure and point out to Jerry how developing trust and value make the selling process so much easier. This was a great example of that for Jerry.

"Jerry, we talked earlier about product knowledge as being the easiest and probably the quickest way to make progress in earning the respect of a customer. Remember?"

"Yes, I do."

"When it comes to generating sales, pricing is the low hanging piñata as well. I hear constantly, that our prices are too high. The competition is a lot cheaper, and it saves them money. Depending on the industry, price may drive sales results. I can't argue the point. However, much more than less, price is not the only main point in the discussion."

"Then what is? Jerry asks.

"Quality and service!"

"There is an adage about this. 'I can give you best price, best quality, or best service. Which two do you want?' And it is still true. It's why we have competition. It's usually true that companies can't provide all three consistently."

"It sure makes logical sense to me, I can tell you that," Jerry responds.

"What I am saying is that there will be so many situations you will experience with customers wanting a lower price. Be careful on how you respond. If you get in the habit of thinking that low prices are all we have for solutions, your game is over. Build quality into your performance and know intimately your strong points. Know all of your benefits and be able to recite them if someone wakes you up at 2AM and asks for the recital."

"OK," is all poor Jerry could come up with.

As the men get into the car Les opens up his call sheets and makes several notes. He is writing intently almost to the point of being isolated. Several minutes pass and Jerry starts to feel uncomfortable. "This isn't like the way this trip has been so far….why is Les all of a sudden being so withdrawn?" Jerry is thinking.

After a few more moments and another page an a half of notes Les finally looks up.

"Sorry Jerry, I didn't mean to ignore you. It is so important to me to record the meetings I have with customers. If I don't, I have nothing to base my next calls on. I have been this way my whole career, and I am so used to travelling by myself, I almost forgot you were here. Please, don't take offence to that comment; it's just how I have conditioned myself and my call routines."

"I'm sure glad to hear that. For a minute I thought you were writing up the summary to my 'walking papers.'"

"Heck no, you are doing great. You did a good job of listening in there. I'm glad you're on this trip."

"Thanks Les, that means a lot."

"So, is your memory so bad that you have to write all of that information down, just to remember that we made a call?" Jerry asks in a semi joking way.

"No, I could wing it and try to remember what needs to be done for them. I don't document this much on every call, but I needed to get some ideas and thoughts recorded about this upcoming proposal for Max. I could just go on to the next stop and wait until tonight to try and make all of my documentation. But, half of the important details would disappear, and it would be such a backlog at night, I would lose valuable rest."

"Wow Les, you really are committed to this job aren't you?"

"It's a decision that we all get to make Jerry." Les is holding fingers up as he is responding.

"First of all, we can choose to be marginal at what we do. Or, we can be very good at what we do. The most favorable choice is that we can be the best at what we do. I made the decision a long time ago to be the best I can be. Creating a plan, as well as organizational structures and habits, I can do my job very effective, and not bring it home at night to my family. Does that make sense?"

"Oh yeah, it makes a lot of sense. However, I don't think there are very many salespeople out there that take to heart a total commitment to perform like you do. So far, it has been very impressive."

Jerry is starting to feel pretty good about this week travelling with Les. He is generating some motivation for himself, and Les's actions are moving Jerry in a very positive direction. Not to mention, Les is certainly enjoying the student, as well as the attention from a newbie.

"I appreciate that comment Jerry, I really do. It's good to hear that someone may learn from some of my experience without making the mistakes I have."

As Les pulls out of the parking lot he finds his favorite Rock channel on the radio and cranks it up real high. He then starts slapping his hands on the steering wheel to the beat of Kiss's 'Rock & Roll All Night.' Jerry looks surprised, but just laughs and joins in.

Chapter Four

CHAPTER FIVE

"You know Les, the thing I wonder about is if I will ever gain the customers total trust. Maybe it's just because I am new and haven't had the experience and the face to face conversations yet. It seems like it is such an intimate interaction."

"Empathy really helps a lot when talking to customers. It is a very big deal in our profession. Customers and prospective customers will get a quick feeling as to why you are in their 'space.' Your actions will speak that purpose loudly. Many times it will be a subconscious action. Are you there for them, or are you just looking to get an order?"

Jerry forms a questionable look on his face.

"So if I walk into a business, and everyone is crying, I need to cry as well, even though I know nothing about what they are crying about?"

"Exactly, and then run out the door and get flowers." Les is glancing at Jerry to see if he is paying attention. Then he grins.

Jerry looks back at Les and says, "Do you think roses are appropriate in most cases, or should I bring back a flower that they can plant?" He then slaps his hand on the dash of Les's car and gives les a strange look.

"I was just checking to see if you were following along buddy."

"Don't worry Mr. Brigham, I'm taking it all in. You just keep 'preaching' and I'll stay awake."

"Now back to what we were talking about. Empathy is an emotion that can be faked, but be careful with it. Don't practice faking empathy. Your customer will figure it out. Just be careful here, and remember the discussion prior about being genuine and confident? Build your customer relationships on being genuine."

"I'm not a very good actor Les. I don't think I could fake any real deep emotions if I tried."

"Knowing you so far, I don't think you could either."

Les continues.

"This also intertwines with the whole customer service thing as well. Always back up your great image with great actions. If you even hint that you will do something for a customer, be sure and follow through with the task. It proves your sincerity, and speaks volumes about how you serve your customers."

Jerry has been writing notes like a mad man. He is flipping papers like a card shuffler at a Las Vegas Casino.

"The world is full of salespeople that promise the world, and then fall short on delivery. If you or your company can not perform, don't suggest that you can. Also, don't promise, and then run with the concept knowing that your company will fall short and you can blame it on them. In your customer's eyes, you fell short. You can't hide behind the organization you work for when it comes to poor performance. You are your company!"

"I'm getting it Les, I'm getting it."

Another hour of watching pavement move under the tires of Les's car and they are approaching their second stop.

"What's the 'M.O.' on this company Les. Big customer, or just a prospect?"

"This is one of my regular accounts. They purchase quite frequently, and have a great deal of loyalty. I haven't been calling on them for a long while, maybe a year at best. I'm still learning about them."

"Ross Epstein is the Plant Manager here. He's a fairly straight shooter, and I shoot straight with him as well. Not a lot of levity in his position and it shows in his personality."

"Some days he is somewhat congenial, and other days he won't even see me. I have watched him 'go postal' on a couple of his people. It's not a pretty sight. I use extreme caution with him, but I am by no means afraid of him. And I don't say that in a macho way, I just understand what my position is in our relationship and keep everything in perspective."

Les and Jerry proceed to the receptionist.

"How's Les today," came the voice of Julie Haldren, the receptionist for Waterman Enterprises.

"Couldn't be better if I tried. You look stunning as always."

"You are such a charmer, someday I will believe you."

Julie was interrupted by one of the sales people in back of her. She turned around to address the interruption and then turned back to Les, almost distracted.

"Is Ross in?"

"Well let's just find out."

"Ross, Les Brigham with ContainPro is here to see you....are you available?" Her voice asks cautiously, as if she knows the personality of Mr. Epstein.

"Thank you sir, I will send them back."

She motions them to proceed to Ross's office. "I know you know where he is."

"I sure do. You have yourself a great day Julie." Les says, as he and Jerry head back.

"How are things going this morning Ross?" Les asks.

"Not too bad for a Monday Les. Who is this, your replacement?"

"Ross, this is Jerry Feldman. He will be joining our sales team in a few months. He will replace one of our more seasoned veterans when he retires."

Ross gets out of his chair and shakes Jerry's hand.

"Are you getting in some windshield time with the road warrior? You're probably just keeping him company, or is this a training trip?"

Jerry responds. "It's a training trip, which by the way I am actually enjoying."

"That's great. You are working with a real professional. Pay attention and you will learn a lot."

"I know," Jerry responds. "I'm staying awake."

"Les, anything going on that I need to know about? Are there any bargains or specials this month?" Ross inquires.

"We are offering 20% off on all consumable supplies this month. We mailed a gloss sheet to all of the accounts. Do you remember seeing it Ross?"

"Oh yeah, and here is a PO for some other items. We were fairly well stocked up so the order isn't very big. Sorry."

"No problem Ross, did you happen to see the notice on special price dating on orders over $10K?"

"Yeah I did. What do you think Les, have you been getting much play on that with any other accounts?"

"You know Ross, it's a good deal for some companies that the big purchases work for, but your consumable needs are in the amounts that a huge order like that just for dating, may not be a good move."

"That's what I was thinking as well. I would need to buy 2 years worth to total that amount, and it wouldn't pay. I'm glad you thought that too." Ross says.

"I was thinking about that on the way up here. The only way it would be beneficial is if you bought for your other locations and had us drop ship. Would you consider anything like that Ross? Or could you?"

Les was always looking for ways to make a sale, but it should be predicated as beneficial to the customer in some way.

"You know Les, consumables are consumables. They get used up. That's why they are called consumables. Quality and longevity is not a big factor. We buy the bulk of those types of products from deep discount suppliers and save ourselves money from the purchase. I really don't think you can compete with the companies we buy most of that stuff from currently."

"I agree again. I just needed to mention it. No harm in asking. "

"You never leave any stones left unturned Les. I can always count on that."

"It looks like today this PO is all you get. I'll be sure and call you if anything comes up."

"Thanks Ross, I appreciate it. We'll get going and let you get on with your day. Thanks for the business."

"Jerry, keep an eye on this guy. Don't let him get out of line."

"No worries there Ross. Will do."

"Take care."

The men do the ceremonial hand shake, and Les and Jerry continue on their journey.

They were walking back to the car as Jerry asks Les.

"Do any of our promotions actually sell product for us Les?"

"Oh yeah, usually. There just wasn't anything we offered for Ross."

"But isn't it important to get your customers to buy into your specials?" Jerry asks, almost just to keep the topic in play.

"Here's the deal with that Jerry."

"As employees of sales organizations we get pulled in many different directions. Our company taunts a new promotion that they want us to believe is the best thing since pull top beer cans. In time you will be able to decide if it is a good deal to promote, and who to promote it to."

"Program offerings from our organization vary monthly. Some salespeople will understand the benefit if there is one and others will clam up and pretend like it doesn't exist. That is the way promotional programs go. One isn't for everyone, and if you try to influence a customer with a program or special that you don't believe in, you will hurt your self with your customer. You will look like a trained monkey, and there are plenty of them out there already."

"I get it, just asking."

It's into the early afternoon, and Les hasn't stopped for lunch as of yet.

"We need to get something to eat. I'm sorry we haven't done it sooner. There are days that eating takes a back seat on the priority list, and it just hurts my concentration."

"What do you want to eat?"

"I really don't care, but see if we can find something somewhat healthy."

During lunch, Les keeps his momentum going with Jerry. This is a learning trip, and he is going to try to get as much information in Jerry's mind that he can.

"Hey Les, I know that the plan is for me to take over Ken's territory when he retires. I am assuming that I will have a very well groomed list of accounts."

"Maybe, or maybe not. Some organizations will take a personnel change in the field as an opportunity to change accounts around. ContainPro is no exception."

"They will probably take the more trouble free or conditioned accounts and make them 'house accounts.' Then they will take another look at Ken's territory and see if any of his accounts require a more advanced or knowledgeable representative. Chances are they could move some of those as well."

"Really" Jerry questions. I will probably get just a lot of scrap accounts, or non producers then?" For the first time Les saw concern in Jerry's eye's.

"I don't think that it will be all that bad. Dirk will probably work with you on a lot of it. Depends on how confident he feels you are with working with the accounts Ken has."

"How's he going to know what I can do without any experience seeing these folks to begin with?"

"He'll know, and he will also most likely ask those of us that have worked with you in your training phases."

Les continues.

"An organization like ContainPro, or any organization places a high value on the revenue stream that come from their customers. It's not a personal thing if they pass a valuable account to a veteran salesperson. Customers get used to dealing with an organization and dread the thought of 'training' a new representative."

"I understand that Les, I really do. I'm sure they want as little amount of change when a salesperson quits calling on them."

"A lot of these businesses have aligned themselves with our company. They trust us, and they trust the person that is taking care of them. Bringing in a new guy makes them uneasy, because they don't know them. However, a well qualified and well trained salesperson can move right into the previous person's role with little issue, if done right."

"Les, I'm not sure if you know how my compensation plan is going to work. It sounded to me like I will get paid on commissions from sales I make. My first 'fantasy' was that I would have a very well groomed base of business that would net me a decent income. Now I'm concerned it will be a bit different."

"Jerry, I wouldn't worry about that issue at all. If you go after this career with a decent plan, and keep working it and modifying it for the better, you will be up and running in no time."

"You also will have to groom some of your less productive accounts. Some of those that are buying little from us now may need to be shown the benefits of working with you. That's where you will get to make a name for yourself. The company knows that you will do that as well. That's how we grow as an organization."

"In your opinion then Les, what do you think my initial plan should be?"

"To begin with, see as many individuals as you can. But, be consistent with your message."

"As a new salesperson your goal is to self promote. If a company promotes your exposure in your territory for you, it helps, but people still need a solid hand shake and a direct look in the eyes. ContainPro will help a little on the promotion but not as consistent as you can do on your own."

"You'll need to go out and introduce yourself like there is not one day to waste. Start the process of learning about your customers and prospective customers."

"When you do this it may be best to have a patented well rehearsed 'message' sketched out. Not like a boring, and dull canned presentation, but an outline that you need to be very familiar with. And then style flex with each customer, but cover the topics in your plan. This needs to be flexible, yet organized and polished."

"Not like someone at a carnival selling super sponges?" Jerry jokes.

"No, not at all. When I say polished, I don't mean phony, or one-sided. I mean polished as in knowing every word, or paragraph, or sentence. This way you can get interrupted and still know what else you need to say. You won't always have the opportunity to talk about everything you feel you need to."

"And yes, I know that this sounds very one sided."

"It sure does." Jerry responds. "Now you are telling me that it's all about me and not about them?" You're sending out mixed messages. First it was listening, now it's talking."

"It may seem that way I understand."

"From experience. If I have customers with 'listening ears,' it means they are interested in what I have to say. You must watch carefully to see if you are educating them about your organization or your services, or just showing them that you know how to talk. They don't care about your talking talent. So watch out for their time and if you are imposing on them draw the "educating" to a close. If you are taking up their time, against their will, you are doing much more harm than good, even if your commodity is free. They will not look forward to your return."

"Isn't a part of this relationship listening to the customers? Jerry interjects again."

"It is one of the most important parts. And, I will promise you it will be one of the most challenging things to learn especially early on."

"I can see how it could. When I get excited about something, I just want to talk about it. I guess I take on the role of an evangelist about my company. It's probably not good. I'll have to watch that." Jerry says with deep thought.

"It's OK to be jazzed about your company. Just remember about the 'radio station' analogy. They want to know what is in the conversation that benefits them, but they really move toward you when you ask questions. I can't over emphasize that point."

"Once you get to know your customers and you become 'business friends' you can share more and more. They will listen a lot more as well."

"You know Les, with my previous employer I used to sit in on a lot of sales meetings. Not all were required, but a few. Do you know what our sales manager was advising our sales developers to do?"

"What?"

"He told our guys that the best way to get to know an account was to go in and stay there at least for an hour on every call. Their challenge was to walk in the door and try and engage them in conversation for at least an hour. I'm not sure that seems effective, not to mention courteous to the customer."

"That was 'old' sales mentality. And it worked well back when the pace was slower, technology was in its infancy and there was a checkerboard set up on the counter. I would never think of trying a technique like that today."

"There are times when I spend a lot more than an hour talking with an account, but it is because I am welcome there, and not just trying to waste our time together, and sample their coffee. As you get established with your customers, you will naturally spend a lot more time with them. The challenge will be actually to get away, not hang around for any required length of time."

"Yeah, I didn't buy into the theory when they were talking about it, and I sure don't today."

Lunch is finally served, and the two men enjoy a great meal talking on more personal topics.

Chapter Five

CHAPTER SIX

It's about mid afternoon and Les has one prospecting stop to make. This is a very important process that he really wants to get Jerry knowledgeable with.

"You see this company up here on the right? I've been meaning to stop in and check them out for a long time. We are going to do it today. It couldn't be better timing."

"Great, it will be interesting to see you walk into a business as a stranger, as opposed to a member of their team, or known well."

"This is one place I should have been in a long time ago. Here is the entry plan."

"Knowing little about what they do, but making a fair guess, I'm going to go through my literature supply and find a few interesting sheets that could be of interest to them. I'm going to put this information into one of our pocket literature folders with a business card. I may be way off on my hunches here but I want to take in something."

"All right." Jerry responds.

"We'll cover this more but when I get out of the car, I make sure that I am happy or thinking of something pleasant. If I go in that building, thinking about something negative, it will precede my presence, and I will send a poor first message. This is a crucial part of a very first call."

"So, do you tell yourself a joke and laugh as you are getting out of the car or tickle yourself with a feather?" Jerry asks laughing.

"I try several things, and usually find something that works. Start to write down crazy stuff that you find funny. Don't overlook using cheat sheets to get your mind engaged. It's all legal, as long as you project friendliness."

Les looks at Jerry and says, "I'm taking you with me on this call, but if you screw it up for me I'm making you sit in the car the rest of the day. And you can't listen to the radio either.

Both men are laughing.

"Exit car now!" Les yells.

They walk in the front door with a grin on their face, just as Les wanted.

They are greeted by the receptionist.

"May I help you," she asks.

"You may be able to help me, but this guy with me is beyond help," Les throws out.

"Well, its Monday afternoon, you guys should be on the downhill slide of getting the first day of the week out of the way," she continues.

"We're on the downhill slide all right, probably in more ways than one." Jerry adds to the banter.

Les get closer to the counter, and introduces himself.

"I'm Les Brigham with ContainPro, and this is Jerry Feldman. I have been meaning to stop in here for a long time, and today just happens to be your lucky day." Les states in a joking way.

"Well, we feel honored," the receptionist responds in a cheerful tone.

Les smiles.

"Who is the person that would be in charge of ordering these types of materials for you organization?" Les shows her one of the brochures in his folder.

"That would be Jessica Slade. Do you want me to see if she could see you? She is always busy, but she may take the time."

"That would be great, thank you." Les responds.

The lady calls Jessica's office.

"Thank you Jessica," the receptionist replies.

"She will come out to see you. You guys got lucky."

"And we appreciate it to, believe me," Jerry responds.

Les is starting to see that Jerry is certainly not shy, and becomes part of the process very well so far.

"I'm Jessica Slade," states a middle aged woman with wire frame glasses. "How can I help you."

Les introduces him and Jerry again.

"Jessica, this is purely a very impromptu stop, and it wasn't meant to interrupt your day. We represent ContainPro." Les says this as he knows everyone is aware of his company.

"I just wanted to get some information in your hands about our company as well as a line card of the items we manufacture and represent. Do you have time to chat for a moment, or is this a bad time?"

"You probably know the answer to that question already, don't you Les?"

"Based on my experience making cold calls, I am guessing that you are buried with previous commitments. I appreciate you even coming out to greet us."

"It's no problem guys, I have been in your shoes before, and I try to make every effort to listen to a vendor if they are one of value. I'm surprised you haven't been in sooner. ContainPro is a big player in your arena. We aren't exact fits for your products but I will be happy to look at your material."

"Thank you Jessica, we appreciate it. Could I just point one thing out that is included in this material that just slips through the cracks?"

"Sure"

"These are our billing terms, and on this page is our shipping schedule. You'll notice that we have deliveries to this area every other day. Many people in this part of the state find that valuable."

"That's good to know Les, and I will be sure and look over the material. I see you have included a card. Is your cell phone number on the card?"

"It sure is Jessica. Again, I really appreciate your time."

"Thank you as well for stopping by. If I see something of interest, I will be calling you. You guys have a great rest of your day."

"Thank you, we will."

The men say goodbye to the receptionist and head out the door.

"That was a fairly good call, don't you think Les?"

"Yes, I agree. You never know how you will get received. I'll follow this call up with either a letter or phone call, and probably both. My goal is to be able to sit down with her and just find out more about the structure of the company and how they function. That is how we become part of their organization, and how business and vendor relationships are formed."

"On a first call I am so paranoid about imposing. Imposing on a customer is a big hole that I don't ever want to step into."

"You will never know where your customer's attention is focused when you walk in that door. That holds true even if you have made and appointment. Every visit will be unique, and each one should be conducted appropriately and with that thought in mind."

"Again, I am so over sensitive when it comes to imposing. I have been on the other side of the desk, and I always dreaded some person coming by my desk, throwing a pitch at me. Especially, if I had a phone in one ear, and two people on hold."

"Here is what you want to remember:

"Know why you are there."

"Don't' force your way in."

"Don't try to crowd your way in hoping you will have a listening ear."

"Watch for signs of welcoming you."

"I am really enjoying this Les. I hope you are finding value in this trip as well."

"This business is my livelihood. I can talk about it for days. I especially enjoy it when I have someone that is interested in learning about the profession. It's exciting."

"Believe me, I can tell that Les."

"OK, one more stop and it is about 45 minutes away. We're going to see Curley."

"That's great. I've always wanted to meet one of the Stooges."

"Curley is certainly not a stooge, but is fun to see. You'll enjoy it."

On the way, Jerry asks more questions.

"Les, if this is your livelihood, do you ever take this job too personal?"

"I don't think there is a way we can do our jobs without taking it personal. It has to be personal in order to create the drive to continually perform. I think that either way it's a gray area. Your customer must realize that you are doing your job well from a very personal interest. If they think that you are just doing a job for an income, you may let them down when times get tough, or at inconvenient times."

"OK."

"We must be flexible as well. And we must be on our game every day, and react in a positive manner at the drop of a hat, or the ring of a phone. It can be stressful."

"But it's only business, right?" Jerry tosses out.

"I have heard many times, 'It's only business, lighten up.' My business is about me, and that makes it personal. I have witnessed individuals that try to succeed in the sales arena without making it personal. They don't last long."

"I suppose that to do well at anything, you must have a personal stake in it." Jerry responds.

"Just understand that your success is personal, just like getting oxygen is to life. It is not required that you breathe, it just depends on if you want to live or not. The balancing act can be tough at times. It depends on your type of personality as to how you deal with it. I don't regard this job as my hobby."

"I can see how a person's expectations can have a lot to do with their success as well." Jerry adds.

"Oh yeah, think about it. Some people work in very routine jobs everyday with a fixed income. They have adjusted their life and expectations knowing that their advancement or growth will come through hourly increases, or promotions. They understand the playing field and are able to separate the job from the personal life. At times I am envious."

"I know people like that."

"I do to Jerry, many people like that."

"This sales career is about thinking constantly about how to create the next sales relationship. How to get to understand the next prospective customer, learn about their needs and help them. It is not an 8 to 5 position. And it is definitely personal."

Jerry is turning note pages and looking at his list of topics to discuss.

"Les, what's the deal about quota. I know what it is and how it works, but why such a stressful topic to so many?"

"It's probably the way so many management personnel use it as a sharp stick to keep jabbing their sales staff. In many instances the 'quota thing' takes on a life of its own, and can be looked as an adversary instead of a common goal."

"ContainPro is no different. At least it hasn't been in the past. Quota was a hammer, and we were the nails. And we both now how that relationship works."

"In the fast pace of many sales companies there are many requirements in place for the advancement or success of their sales staff. One of those requirements is that word called 'quota.' It can be scary, or it can be understood and dealt with intelligently."

"Would you like my spin on this Jerry? You're going to get it anyway, you realize that." Les produces his familiar smile.

"Oh yeah, I'm ready for it. Lay it on me."

"Companies know how much revenue they must produce to create a thing called profit. Profit is what pays the bills of the company. Some people think that just sales do that, but it is what's left over that takes care of the overhead. Many times quotas are set based on required amounts of income. These required amounts of income produce the required amount of profit to pay the bills and produce growth in the company."

"Then why don't they just call it what it is, a freaking requirement?"

"Hell, I don't know. Probably because of some legal ramifications and being able to retain or dismiss individuals based on performance. Who knows?"

"The real issues arise when the 'quota thing' becomes the biggest thing. Quota chasing and quota pressure can be big burdens. Having a bad year and not making quota for your team can be grueling on our mindset."

Jerry quickly interjects. "I can see where it would make some individuals a bit crazy, that's for sure."

"Oh yeah, that's when less than perfect decisions are made by some. The pressure that comes from having the quota requirement over your head has lead many of 'less than confident' sales people make 'less than honest' decisions. Don't get caught in the trap of thinking that you have to acquire sales by unethical methods just to make quota."

"I kind of hold a higher image of myself than to turn to dishonest actions." Jerry assures Les. "What should a person do when things are just not happening even though you are working you tail feathers off trying to make things happen?"

"What has worked well for me is that in troubling times, or in an unusual sales slump I stay in constant contact with my manager and be sure he knows of my efforts. I listen to their suggestions if offered and I keep trying. Communication during weak sales cycles can help you keep your position, and reduce stress."

CHAPTER SEVEN

It's time to go see Curley. Les has said just enough about Curley to make Jerry very curious.

Les and Jerry walk in the front door of CHL Enterprises. A voice shouts across the room.

"Hey Brigham, whose your shadow? I knew that they were going to send a chaperone along with you eventually!"

Les knew who it was. He knew the voice distinctly. It was Merle Crawford, the President of CHL.

Les just raised his hand and pointed to Merle as to say, "You are correct, this guys is my chaperone."

Then he yelled back.

"I'm glad to see they finally let you out, or did you just break out? I knew that there wasn't an institution in existence that would keep you very long."

The last thing that anyone could do was to throw out a smart comment to Les Brigham, and not expect to get it back in their face tripled.

Les walked over to Merle, Jerry at his side.

"Mr. Crawford, it's good to see you, really. What are you doing in the office today, I thought that Monday was your day of classes at the Nursing Facility?"

Les continued. "Merle, this is Jerry Feldman. He's a new employee and will soon be out doing what I do."

Merle looks at Jerry.

"Are they going to pay you for that service, or do you have to pay them?" Merle was exhibiting a wide grin.

"I'm hoping to get paid. At least that is what our agreement was." Jerry quipped.

"I'm sure you will Jerry. ContainPro is a very reputable organization. It's just too bad you have to learn from this guy." Merle points to Les.

Les jumps in the conversation. He looks at Jerry and says jokingly, "And why did we come in here again?"

"If I remember, it was to see someone named Curley."

"Well then, I have done my part in getting you warmed up. You better get back there. You don't want to keep her waiting."

For an instant Jerry was surprised. He was assuming that Curley was a guy.

"Merle, you have a wonderful day! And by the way, thank you for your continued business."

"It is always a pleasure to see you Les, always a pleasure. Jerry, have fun hanging out with this guy. You should learn a lot. And by the way, it was nice meeting you."

"Thanks Merle. I'm hoping to. I'm thinking that before we are finished we'll run across someone that likes him."

"Good luck with that one buddy." Merle chuckles and walks into his office.

Les motions for Jerry to follow him back to Curley's office.

"Hi Pricilla, how are you on this wonderful Monday afternoon?"

Pricilla is a very interesting person. She is a rather robust lady, wearing a skin tight yellow dress with a very high hemline. She has shiny orange boots that come up to her knees. Black lipstick and a ring pierced through her left nostril. Heavy eye makeup and thick foundation. But her most noticeable feature is her hair. Most of her head is shaved with a mousse star pattern Mohawk.

At first glance, you would be cautious and not sure how to approach her. She looked more like a circus act than an employee of a reputable company.

"It doesn't get any better than this. I am happy to be alive!" she answers.

"Pricilla, this is Jerry Feldman, he is my 'co-pilot' on this trip. He will eventually have his own territory and I am getting the chance to show him some of the ropes."

"It's nice to meet you Jerry, and if Les hasn't told you, my nickname is Curley. You can call me that as well."

"Great, Curley, it's nice to meet you."

"Did Les bring you by, just to see his most controversial customer?"

"No, I don't think so. He did promise me though that I would be entertained."

"So, that's what you call working with me Les, entertained?" She asks in a friendly, sarcastic tone.

"You have always entertained me P.C., and not just because of your unique presence."

"And I'm OK with that as well," she responded.

"Not to change the subject Mr. Brigham but I found something out about your company's 6700 Micro-bond Chromium Re-sealers."

"Really?" Les responded.

"I did some studying on the product and I found out that I could get a titanium alloy product for about 40 percent less cost, and it proves to be about 50 % more efficient and less of a chore to maintain. I have been getting them from Campmore, and the savings have been fairly significant."

"You know, I was wondering why we haven't been moving as many of those. It's actually a product that we outsource, and it is represented by a completely different company. I just have it in my sales box. It's a fairly technical device, and I haven't really taken the time to learn much about how it fits in to our offerings. Shame on me."

"Don't sweat it dude, I just want you to know I'm awake and watching my part of the circus around here. I'm not busting your buns."

Les responds by talking with Jerry.

"Jerry, this lady is one of the smartest and 'dialed in' individuals that I call on. I come by here not only to see how I can help her, but to get information on the industry, and some of my products. I have probably learned more from this girl, than any of my customers. She is always on her game. Don't ever let Dirk know I said that."

"How many Master's Degrees do you now hold girl?"

"Only four. Some day I am going to go out and find a real job, but I don't think my dad cold manage this all by himself."

"I'm catching on now, Pricilla Crawford, Merle's daughter?"

"That's me. My dad is quite liberal and I appreciate it. He looks beyond my unique presence and let's me contribute based on my talent and contribution to the company."

"Jerry, you should have been here the first day Les met me. He wasn't sure what to think."

"I remember that day well P.C. I didn't know much about you, and your flamboyant appearance really had me wondering."

Les continued. "I remember you were married at the time, and a little more reserved. Your knowledge, and the way you did your job just blew me away. I didn't even know you were Merle's kid until months later. I was mesmerized by how sharp you were."

"Yeah, I had a lot of fun with that back then."

"I remember one day I had a vendor sitting in my office and my dad had just went out and picked up my new car. I had already done the deal, and he was just picking it up for me."

"Do you remember this story Les?" Pricilla asks.

"Oh yeah, you got up and went over and put your arms around your dad and said something like, 'Thank you for the new car daddy, I'll try to be a lot nicer from now on.' If I remember right, your dad walked out of your office and you made some comment about how you were such a spoiled little brat."

Pricilla finishes the story. "Yeah, that guy from Bodman just sat there expressionless."

"You're quite unpredictable P.C., that's some of your beauty. It goes along with your orange hair. By the way, I really liked it green."

Jerry is just standing there watching the interaction between Les and Pricilla. He is amazed at how they seem to be such good friends.

"Do you have anything for me this trip P.C.?" Les asks.

"Oh yeah." Pricilla opens up her desk drawer and hands Les a printed purchase order with about 10 items on it. Les scans it for any unusual items and thanks her for the order.

"This is just another reason I like you. You know what you want, and I don't have to do any work."

"You have earned it Les. You taught me a thing or two about inventory control and stock adjustment. Your patent rant 'dust on boxes cost me money.' You pounded that into my head and that's why you were a big influence on how I actually found a passion for this part of dad's company."

"I'm going to see if I can do anything for you in titanium re-sealers. I'll call when, and if I find something."

"Great Les, thanks. I have to get back to my inventory. Had a computer glitch last night, and things just don't look right today. Have found a ton of mistakes, and I am not sure I'm ready to panic or not yet."

"You'll figure it out P.C. You always do."

"We're going to run now. I have to keep Jerry moving, or he falls asleep."

Chapter Seven

Jerry looks at Les, and then at Pricilla.

"Don't worry Jerry," Pricilla says, "I know how he is."

They all chuckle and the two men leave her office.

The work day is drawing to a close as Les and Jerry get into Les's car.

"Where are we staying tonight" Jerry asks.

"It's about another mile from here. It's where our first stop is for the morning. I actually made reservations this time."

Les makes that comment with an unusual tone.

"This time, don't you normally make reservations?"

"I try to, but many times my calls are hard to predict. I may knock out only five stops in a day, or there are times when I complete more than ten. We have an appointment tomorrow in this town so I knew it would be safe to book the rooms. Otherwise I wait until later in the day when I know where I'll be. Does that make any sense?"

"Oh yeah, my dad did that all of the time when he was travelling. There were times he would complain about having to stay in some seedy motel because he couldn't get a room booked later in the day. Believe I know what you are saying."

"Yeah, my wife Cindy always flips me crap about it when I can't find a decent place to stay. She says that I am more concerned about my customers than I am with myself. I never want to tell her that many times she is correct."

"Sounds like if I do this business long enough, I should take occasional 'reality checks' to see where my priorities are. It can get to be a real obsession." Jerry states.

"Oh yeah."

"This is our hotel up here on the right side. I stay here regularly. The rooms are newer, the service is polite, and the internet is fast."

"Is a fast internet a big deal?" Jerry asks puzzled.

"It is when you have to move data back and forth or use our online call reporting software. It can mean the difference of working on work stuff after hours for 30 minutes, or an hour and a half."

"Wow, I didn't think of that. I'll remember that one."

"We're just getting started man, just getting started."

"Jerry, I would strongly suggest that you sign up for awards points with the hotels that you like staying at. You earn points with every stay, and you can redeem them for free nights most anywhere. Ken can help you with that for his, I mean your new area."

"Cool, I can do that."

"We went on a family vacation for two weeks the year before last, and we didn't pay for one hotel stay. We just redeemed points. It was a great savings, and it took no effort."

"I would also suggest that you setup a separate checking account and debit card just for company travel and expenses. You will get reimbursed for your expenses and you don't want it mixed up in you own personal checking or bank accounts. Also, get a credit card that earns points as well. This really adds up fast. It earns points that you can redeem in gift cards or checks."

"May I help you?" the hotel staff member asks.

"Yes, Les Brigham, and Jerry Feldman. You should have reservations for us."

"Let me look. Yes, right here. Will you be keeping these on the same credit card?"

"Yes, please."

Les looks back at Jerry and says, "I'm picking up all of the expenses on this trip, but when they release you out in the world, you'll use your own credit card. It's easier for me to expense everything now, and you will get to go over expense reimbursement during your formal training and orientation to the sales department."

"That sounds good to me Les. Thanks."

The two men get their room cards and proceed down the hall toward the elevator.

"Let's meet down here in about 30 minutes. We'll go out and have some dinner."

CHAPTER EIGHT

"Hi, my name is Gwen, and I will be your server tonight. Can I start you off with an appetizer or something to drink?"

Les orders an iced tea and Jerry a diet soda.

"So, how did your first day feel?"

"It's been fine. I've just got to sit back and watch you do your thing. I've enjoyed it. I'm looking forward to the rest of the trip!"

"I've enjoyed the day as well Jerry. I think that you are going to do fine. You certainly are not afraid to enter into conversations, and are cordial and polite. I sense that you are genuine, and I'm betting that you are honest. I think you should do well."

"Any concerns so far Jerry?"

"No, not really. I have to tell you that I was really thinking that they were going to just give me Ken's accounts, and I knew he was successful so it would be easier for me to make it."

"What do you mean by 'make it'?" Les asks concerned.

"I guess I figured that my income would be fairly substantial from the beginning. You have told me that I will probably only get a portion of Ken's accounts and the higher producers may get handed off to a more senior rep."

"I can see how that could be a shock if you were lead to believe differently. Did someone tell you different?"

"No, I just had talked to friends that kept telling me that when a person takes over an established sales territory much of the income is already onboard. I just have to maintain the accounts and take care of them."

"Were these people you were talking to experienced salespeople?"

"One was, from a few years back. The other guys were just throwing out what they had heard."

"Jerry, here's the deal. Are you familiar with the more common compensation plans out there? You need to know this information. OK?"

"Sure, fill me in."

"Most effective salespeople are paid commissions on what they sell. Remember? It is their reward for producing revenue for the company. Some are very cautious of commission positions as the income can fluctuate a lot. I'm sure this has you concerned."

"Well Les, fluctuating income can raise havoc with consistent bill paying. When there are little funds how can you pay your bills? You can't. It's just that simple."

"Not so fast Sparky, you need to be aware of some techniques that can help you, and also implement some self discipline."

"OK, that won't be an issue."

"Jerry, most companies will not hire a salesperson just to have them go broke and go away. Hiring decisions by companies are most always based on positive expectations. That is why it takes organizations such a long time to make hiring decisions. It is not a fun process for them."

"But before we talk about how to deal with the income fluctuation issues, let's go back and talk about a few other comp plans."

Jerry nods.

"When folks are hired on as salespeople they could have a few compensation scenarios. I know how yours will go with our company, but here are some other basic ones, and doesn't include every diversification."

"First one, a fixed salary. This type of arrangement is good for those that need security of a steady paycheck. However, it leaves no room for income growth, and success on your part is rewarded meagerly if at all."

"Then why would they offer a program like that?"

"A company will offer this type of pay plan if they are established well, and are not aggressive to increasing sales. The company usually has a structured account base, and are not expecting the salesperson to do much more than be a good liaison between them and their customers. I'm not sure why they even call them sales reps."

"Does anything else come with it?" Jerry asks interested.

"Other benefits for the salesperson are included as well like health insurance and maybe even a vehicle they could drive during the day."

"Isn't a fixed salary sales job is like taking a vacation on a train. You are on a set path, and you will only see what is next to the tracks."

"You got it, but there are some people out there that find security in knowing what they can count on for income every month. It's a good fit for some."

"It wouldn't be for me, I can tell you that," Jerry retorts.

"Me either," Les agrees.

"The next compensation scenario will be a salary 'plus' commission. It's the one you will have."

"That's what was discussed during the interview."

"This arrangement is made to give the salesperson a sense of security and the incentive to grow the business. It is one of the more common compensation packages out there."

"The salary is usually mediocre, and the commission percentage is usually decent, as well as bonuses for achieving set dollar totals for months, or the year. This usually comes with benefits as well and quite possibly car allowance or even a company furnished vehicle. This compensation plan is created to provide incentive for being active and productive."

"And the last one I will mention is the "straight commission" program. No base pay. Probably no vehicle or car allowance."

"Why would anyone want that one Les? It sounds scary."

"Well, the commission structure is fairly liberal and it allows you to create a very decent income. But remember, you only get paid on what you sell. You could have the standard benefits with this job as well. Your purpose is to generate revenue for your company by selling their products or services. It's almost like being a private contractor, but with benefits."

"I'll bet you there are not many of those out there."

"You would be surprised. It's a very common pay plan for salespeople."

"Wow, I never would have thought."

"As I said earlier, companies don't want to hire a salesperson and then lose them because they can't earn a living. A lot of effort goes into training and orientation and testing. And a lot of expenses are involved as well. Again, that's why hiring decisions take so long."

Jerry continues to nod agreeing. He is getting hungry, and it's starting to show.

"Are you ready to order now?" The waitress asks.

The men order their meals and continue talking.

"To help a new hire get established in the territory many organizations will offer an initial period of time providing a mutually agreed upon salary that keeps the new salesperson solvent while building and getting established in the territory."

"I'm sure that they will do that with you. Did they discuss that earlier?"

"Yes, 90 days on a fixed income, then I go to my reduced base, and the added commissions."

"I think that these companies understand that it is hard enough trying to get established as a representative, you certainly don't need money issues weighing on your mind."

"That's exactly how it was discussed with me." Jerry interjects.

"I don't think you will get rich on the initial compensation package either but it should be enough to keep the wolf away from the door at home."

"Write this down please and don't forget it."

Les is looking very intense at Jerry.

"During this time, don't be lazy! Comparing this to flying an airplane, this is your runway time to get up to flying speed. Don't cut back on the throttle. It will be fine, just don't panic, and 'keep the pedal to the metal.'"

Jerry got up to use the restroom and while he was gone Les pulled out his Blackberry and checked his email. Frank Winman had sent him a message. Frank was advising him that he was putting together all of the material that the legal folks needed. He also added reassurance to Les that this will be a very good business for them to be stepping into.

Frank surely wasn't what you would call a veteran entrepreneur. He shared a very similar career path as Les. Jumping into running a small multi-million dollar enterprise was an event that quite honestly still had him spinning.

Sarah Layman-Winman grew up having a resourceful, multi-talented father in Herb Layman. She saw the long hours, and the family alienation that came along with the exhausting journey of developing a successful company. This was comforting in some ways for Frank's mind but he also knew that he really didn't have the interest, or the desire to maintain and continually grow the newly inherited enterprise. Sarah had been through enough as well, and both she and Frank were in common assent with their future plans.

Knowing Les Brigham as a resourceful, forward thinker as well as an honest and trustworthy friend gave Frank some temporary comfort promoting the new changes.

When Jerry got back to the table, the meals arrived. They each ordered another beverage, and enjoyed the rest of the meal not discussing work.

CHAPTER NINE

Jumping into a unique and unfamiliar business venture was surely not something that Cindy Brigham had dreamed about. She was comfortable with watching her husband achieve success in his chosen sales career. However, deep in her mind the thought of her and Les operating their own business had always twinkled in her mind.

Over the years she had watched the grueling sales arena beat her husband into submission several times. She had watched him write his resignation letter, just to file it in a drawer and never put it to use.

She remembered the cold winter morning that Les's boss and best friend John Kershin put a gun in his mouth and bid goodbye to his over stressed life and inimical career. She remembered the change that took place in her husband and how she truly worried for the first time how he was going to make it.

He really never did return to the man she once knew. The Les Brigham that broke almost every sales record for Morphics, Inc, as well as help build a competitive, world class organization that Morphics, Inc still is.

She remembers the day that he finally did open up the file on his computer and pull out one of the many drafted resignation letters. How he printed it, signed his name and carefully folded it up and placed it in the envelope. She remembers his shaking hands and his dry mouth and them both thinking that he was taking the "leap of faith" of a lifetime by accepting a similar position with Morphics strongest competitor. How he felt as a traitor to a company that employed him during the first 25 years of their marriage. The years of watching their children being born, growing up and most now married.

And now, they were about to leave the comfort and accustomed life that they had lived and step into yet another unknown.

The only comforting thing that kept going through Cindy's mind was that this opportunity was quite unique. Unique in the fact that they were not entering into Layman and Sons in the fashion that you would normally enter a business.

Frank Winman trusted Les Brigham. Frank Winman wanted out. He also knew that Les could step into the helm of the company and create a future for him and Cindy beyond belief.

This wasn't a purchase as normal. It was actually an agreement between both couples that Les Brigham would step in as CEO and oversee the daily operations. As a reward Les and Cindy earned ownership in the company at an alarming rate. The plan was that if Les continued at the helm for 10 consecutive years while producing stipends for the Winman's, Layman and Son's would be signed over in it's entirety to Les and Cindy Brigham. They could at that point continue to run the business or sell it. It was theirs to do with what they wanted.

****

Another pleasant morning on the 'Journey of Knowledge' for Mr. Jerry Feldman.

As the men were eating breakfast this morning the topic of expenses came up.

"In your opinion Les, what is the best way to deal with the ups and downs of a commission job? That is probably my biggest fear taking on a 'real' sales position. I am really comfortable with knowing how much money I have coming in every month, and I can plan accordingly."

"That concern is very well warranted. And if you don't get a handle on it, you can develop some real bad habits."

Les continued.

"How do you take care of bills currently? Do you just watch your checking account balance and spend until it is low, or do you actually have a savings account with regular contributions. And I'm not asking this to be too personal, it is just a question."

Jerry responded.

"I'm actually a nut when it comes to paying my bills. I know where every dollar is and when it goes out. Again, that may be why inconsistent paychecks may freak me out. It's a security thing."

"I understand and I have a couple of suggestions."

"First, this is a good time to analyze your spending habits as well as cash flow. Really document what your regular expenses are, as in how much you need for 'survival money' such as food, shelter, and clothing. Determine what that number is right down to the penny."

"OK, then what?"

"In your first few months, you will get a feel for how your money comes in. You will understand the commission structures, draws on commissions, etc., and you will get more comfortable with the whole procedure."

"You really think so Les?"

"Oh yeah. The other thing that you will get to like is the larger than normal paychecks. And you will see many of those as well."

"I'm sure hoping so."

"People get so accustomed to fixed income jobs that they start to live inside of a little pre-built box. It limits their growth, and their livelihood. And unfortunately for many, if not most individuals, it is the best thing for them."

"That's where I am now, I like knowing exactly what my income is going to be. I can plan on things that way."

Les interrupts enthusiastically.

"You can plan on a lot more things when you income starts to increase as well. And believe me, it will happen."

"As you have probably heard, money isn't everything, but it ranks right up there with oxygen."

Jerry shakes his head enthusiastically.

"Spending the time with you that I have already Jerry, I can see how this will be a great fit for you. You may think that you like living inside of a pre-built box, but it could shortly be interpreted as a jail cell. I can see it in your personality. I could be wrong, but I feel that you will do very well!"

"I'm glad you're convinced. I'm getting there as well. I just need a bit of time to realize where I am heading. Your confidence in me helps Les, thanks."

"No problem dude, it will be fine."

"As far as personal finances go how do you manage your bank accounts?"

The answer to this question would tell Les a lot about Jerry.

"What do you mean, manage?"

Chapter Nine

"Do you use a checkbook, or a computer?"

"I use a checkbook. Always have."

"Are you afraid of a computer?"

"No, not at all. I design websites for a hobby."

"A suggestion would be to get an automated program. There are plenty of them out there, but the proven ones are the best, and we can go into that later."

"I have been doing fine with my check book register and my savings passbook."

"Are you serious? I couldn't do it that way if I tried."

"Why couldn't you?" Jerry asked.

"With an automated program I learned to create reserve accounts within a savings account. I had to keep track of the amounts initially on a separate spreadsheet, but eventually I was able to work with my automated program and keep track of it."

"What are reserve accounts in your mind?"

"Reserve accounts are monthly deposits made into an account and you make note as to how much was deposited, and how much was allotted to a particular cause. For example:"

He had Jerry's attention.

"Tires needed for the family car. You may need $450 every 2 years."

"Yeah."

"Each month deposit into a savings account $18.75 for tires. When it comes time to buy tires for the car, you will have the money. In the meantime the money sits in a savings account earning interest, not much I know but the main thing is that it is waiting for you when you need it."

"That's interesting, never thought about major expenses like that. I usually wait for my spring time tax refund for those things."

Les interrupts.

"Keep in mind that what one person labels as a major expense may be pocket change for someone else."

"Waiting for the tax refund to purchase things? So does most everyone else. The sad part is that when that refund does get cashed, you notice I didn't say 'deposited,' other things seem more important. The tires end up getting put on a credit card with a revolving balance and it all cost much more over time."

"Really, it's just all about categorizing your expenses and setting aside money for it."

Les continues. "Again remember. It's also what you categorize as a 'major' expense. Different income levels within families, determine what needs to be saved for. One family could struggle with a $300 expense, while others would not think anything about it. Make sense?"

"Oh yeah, and we need to talk more about that Les, we really do."

"I just have one more comment on the money thing, and how it ties into your occupation."

"What's that Les?"

"It's just money. It pays our bills, and as salespeople we earn it by selling our goods and services. This profession can be a roller coaster ride as compared to a fixed income job. Our paychecks can go from a little weak to extremely large in a short period of time."

Les inhales and then continues.

"When times are slow and we need more income we can think about selling our goods or services in different ways. My advice is to stay grounded. Understand that it is a cycle. Then again if the ride is too unstable for your comfort level then you may need a more stable income producing position."

"However, I really don't think that is your personality. I think you have a lot more to accomplish with your life, as well as developing yourself professionally."

"It's easy for some novice salespeople to focus on the income aspect much more than needed. It is then that representations and promises could be made that may not be accurate. Be careful. As I alluded to earlier, don't let your income requirement damage your ethics.

"I won't Les, don't worry."

"I'm not worried in the least."

"Let's go see a customer Jerry. How about that? We can talk more about this stuff later."

"Let's go, I'm ready."

Les drives into the parking lot of Camperman, Erkins and Holt.

"This place looks and feels more like administrative organization, but they are a great account of mine."

"The name sounds like a group of attorneys."

"Almost, it is an engineering group."

"So, what do you sell them, pencils and rulers?" Jerry asks, almost laughing."

"Wait until you get inside. You will be amazed. These dudes make everything into a model. Rooms and rooms of guys and gals playing with plastic, carving tools, resin, and wood. They use materials and compounds that only a very elite group of design engineers know about not to mention understand."

"Just industrial vacuuming supplies and filters have filled up one whole section of our warehouse."

"Is this the account that buys those big bulky boxes of filters that takes 4 guys to handle?"

"This is one of the accounts, yes."

"And it is quite profitable as well. We made an arrangement to deliver every other day up here and also stock every filter that they use. It has been a very pleasant relationship and we know their business from an internal standpoint. Our warehousing people are on a first name basis with their purchasing folks, and some of them are even close friends.

Myron Simpson is my contact person here. He was instrumental in working with us on this 'partnership.' You will like him as well. Can't wait for you to meet him."

"Remember to smile." Jerry reminds Les with a smirk.

Jerry and Les walk in the front door and greet Janice Greenfield. Janice has known Les for many years, starting back when Les worked for Morphics.

"Hey Lambchop," Les says to Janice.

"The Knight in Shining Armor has arrived. How have you been boyfriend?"

"Absolutely, on top of the world. I couldn't squeeze one more ounce of joy into my heart." Les jokes back.

"I'm really glad to see you got your medication working for you today. It really helps, doesn't it?"

"You better believe it. I couldn't do without them."

They all three laugh.

"Janice this is Jerry Feldman. He is a new employee riding with me this week."

"Hi Jerry, it's nice to meet you. I am so sorry you have to hang out with this bag of wind. How long do you have to be with him?" Janice tries to say without laughing. "Are you driving separate cars?"

"They made me ride with him." Jerry responds while mocking a sad face.

"You are just one laugh after another, Ms. Greenfield. Janice I'm really glad to see you back at work. I'll bet that it was much more serious during this last segment of drug rehab?" This was classical Les Brigham.

Jerry was just taking this all in like he was watching some type of stage performance.

"Brigham, I'm busy. I have a ton of things to get done today and bantering with you 'ain't gettin' me anywhere. Go back and see your little buddy."

Janice came around the corner of her desk and gave Les a big embrace. "Always nice to see you and you know it."

"Same here girl, same here. Oh, before I forget here is the latest picture of Daisy. I had her sign it for you."

Les handed Janice an 8 x 10 picture of the Brigham's Golden Retriever wearing and Easter bonnet. Someone had signed "Daisy" down at the bottom with a little heart design. Daisy didn't look happy.

Janice cracked up laughing.

"This is one of the funniest things I've seen you do with her. She sure doesn't look happy."

"She loved it, until she learned how to flick the whole hat across the room. Some of that green paper grass was in her belly shortly after that picture was taken."

"I'll put it with the rest of my collection. Thanks for the addition."

"You are welcome kid, see you later."

As Les and Jerry were walking down the long hallway to Myron's office they were looking through the big glass doors leading into each design room.

"This is where all of the fun stuff takes place. It's like a crafters paradise." Les tells Jerry.

"I can see if I were a craftsman or model builder, this is where I would love to hang out." Jerry responds.

"These folks in this facility are some of the best in the world. Did you see all of those awards in the front showcase?"

"I did, very impressive."

As they were walking down the hall, the sound of an electric motor was getting louder and louder.

"Get the hell out of the way, or get ran over," came a screeching voice in high octaves. "I got places to go."

With no hesitation Les responds.

"I told you where you ought to go a long time ago, but you were too damn stubborn to listen." Les yells back as a guy in an electric wheelchair with no legs runs right between him and Jerry. The man is laughing but no eye contact was made between them.

"I'll be down in my office with the door locked," the man screams.

"You tried that last time. I just went to the office and got a key. You must have thought up a better 'game' than that by now. Save your self the trouble and just let us in, damn it."

This was a continuation from the first greeting at this company. Jerry was really starting to wonder if they ever got down to business.

"We'll see you in a minute Myron." Les yells as the wheelchair wheels into one of the last rooms on the left.

"I'll be here Les." Myron returns comment.

Les continues to explain to Jerry what seems to be happening in each room as they get closer to Myron's office.

They get to Myron's office and Les just stands at the door and looks at Myron. His office is decorated with lines of plaques and awards. Many military awards and medals.

Then they both break out in a big smile.

"Sit down Les, who's this guy?"

Les waits this time for just a brief moment. Jerry walks over and extends his hand to Myron.

"I'm Jerry Feldman. I'm a new sales person in training."

"Nice to meet you Jerry. Is Les treating you OK?"

"Absolutely awesome, I'm enjoying my time immensely."

"You should, it's always interesting and different to hang out with 'science experiments.'"

"I think I would have liked you more when you were taller." Les throws out.

A stranger hearing someone making a comment to a man that had his legs amputated could be very uncomfortable. But with the way Les interacted with his customers you are assured that he will never say anything that wasn't appropriate for who he was talking to.

"I understand Brigham. I respected you a lot more before you had the stroke. Or whatever you are blaming your inadequacies on this week?"

Jerry broke into a roar of laughter, and Les just smiled.

"Did you see the new construction out in the back part of the campus?" Myron asked Les as he opens up a jar filled with candy, and pops a piece into his mouth.

"No, I didn't notice it. What's happening back there?"

"Another 18,000 square feet of model making. Were hiring 12 new technicians."

"Wow." Les responds. "Same type of filtration?"

"I don't think so. I've heard rumor that they are using some type of 'green' concept. There are probably replaceable parts to it as well, maybe even more, but 'earth friendly.'"

"Who would have that information Myron? I would like to start the research on what it will take, so we can service that facility as well."

"Paul Buxton is the onsite dude. He is the one that appears to have all the answers. Go see him in that little contractor's office/trailer thing before you leave."

"Also, I need a favor Les."

"Sure, what is it?"

"Do you have a little time to edit a usage list for me? I printed it off yesterday and it is grouped by category. I have about 16 pages. Could you glance over it and do a quick edit as to what we use, and don't use?"

"Sounds like you need it for some PA report. How accurate do my edits have to be? Les asks Myron.

"Anywhere close will be fine. I don't want to turn in something that wasn't researched well enough."

Myron turns to address Jerry.

"This is the situation that most salespeople strive for. The customer's purchasing department depending on the salesperson to tell him what they are buying. Luckily, Les has earned the trust, and I don't' have any issue with him having strong input on this."

"I know all I have seen is trusting customers with this guy. He could make a short term fortune, if he was the slightest bit crooked."

"Isn't that the truth, and I have told Les that myself." Myron adds.

As Les looks over the list Myron takes Jerry on a mini inside tour of the facility. He shows him the instrument room, the design suites where the ink and paper plotters create the blueprints for the modelers.

"Now I'll take you where Les makes his money. They go up one floor and walk into a big room. It's dimly lit with hundreds of different size doors and panels. Most of them are circuit boards for the tools that they use. They head back one more door and enter into a room filled with fixtures and cabinets.

"Every one of these doors opens up three filter elements. And behind those, three more. The EPA has us monitored so well because of the composites that we use, we have to keep everything clean and keep the particulates out of the air. We use special compounds that are dangerous if not monitored. We could use different materials, but the finished product would be 'bush league' quality, and that is not why we are world famous."

Myron continues.

"Most of our work is for the aerospace industry. We know what the newest airplanes and parts look like even before the manufacturer does."

"Wow!" is all that Jerry could come up with.

"One last stop and then we'll go back and meet back up with Les."

Jerry walks beside Myron as he travels on his electric wheelchair.

"In case you were wondering, I was in the first Desert 'game' and stepped where I shouldn't have. The bomb was a dud and only partially exploded. That's why I'm still around."

"I'm always curious about things like that. Thanks for sharing."

"No problem. I like to tell folks so they don't spend a lot of time guessing in their minds." Myron states with no hesitation.

Myron leads Jerry down to the supply room. Jerry immediately notices many items that they probably get from Les.

"This is the bulk of Les's offerings for CEH. You could probably ask him to describe this room in his mind, and each shelf and item number would be exact. I have called him before to ask him where we keep certain items and he lead me right to the spot. He did this driving down the road, talking on his cell phone. He knows this facility."

"Nothing surprises me about him, absolutely nothing." Jerry responds.

"I love to give him a bad time whenever he is here because he makes it so much fun. He has a quick wit." Myron states.

"If you can model yourself after Les Brigham, you will do quite well."

"I'm learning that as well Myron."

Jerry and Myron return to Myron's office as Les has finished and is talking on his phone. Les ends the conversation with a concerned tone.

Les Brigham is what one would call quite transparent. When a person has a conversation with Les you are communicating with the whole being. He makes you feel that you are the most important person at that particular moment. Jerry senses something is wrong in Les's world, although Les is doing a good job of covering it up. Something in his aura is a bit dimmer than normal.

"I think that I have it for you buddy. It was actually a fairly easy puzzle referring to the inventory report. I was shocked that I remembered so much of it."

"Hey Myron, did you know that we now offer a software solution that you could integrate into your mainframe and keep track of your supply inventory. We offer it to many of our customers as a free application. The only thing we charge for is installation and training. Support and updates are free."

"More computer programs. Why would I want to do that?"

"So you wouldn't have to rely on me for your answers."

"Maybe someday Les, but for now, I enjoy relying on you. Are you OK with it?"

"Hell yes, that is my driving force. To have my customers rely on me. I just thought you might want better control."

"I'm fine for now Les. Thanks."

"Great, sounds good to me as well, but I am going to keep bringing it up. It's the way of the future for companies like yours."

"Keep bugging me Les, I'm OK with that."

"OK." Do you have anything that you need while I am here?"

"I faxed an order in yesterday afternoon. It's probably being delivered today. Other than that, nothing. I know how to get in touch with you old man, don't worry."

"Be sure and see the Site Manager before you leave the campus to get the specs on the new digs. He is here for about 12 hours a day. I'm surprised I haven't seen him walk in front of my door while you were here."

"Alright Mr. Simpson. I think we're heading over in that direction, and then more stops today."

"Always great to see you Les, keep a close eye on Jerry. He looks shaky." Myron winks at Jerry.

"Thanks for the tour Myron. It was very interesting and nice of you to show me around. Have your self a great rest of the day!"

"I will, take care guys."

Les and Jerry catch up with the onsite guy and are able to get some specs on the new building. Looks like Les will grow this account even more.

Chapter Nine

CHAPTER TEN

Once in the car, Les went back to his note taking, this time trying to keep a conversation with Jerry as he is writing.

"Are you OK Les?" Jerry asks. "I really don't know you very well, but I can sense that you got some disturbing news." Jerry was referring to his phone call.

"I'm OK kid. I just found out something that I wasn't expecting and it has me a bit twisted up. I'll get over it, don't worry."

"OK, I'm sitting right here if you want to talk." Jerry responds.

That comment told Les a lot about this new guy Jerry Feldman. It told him that he was a guy that shows compassion. It is a great asset to have in your portfolio as a sales representative.

"I appreciate it. I have some stuff going on currently that is kind of personal. I have to get a handle on it and then I can share. But right now, I'm still sorting through it. I hope you understand."

"No worries buddy. I just hope you are OK."

Les smiles back.

"Hey Les, can I ask you a question. Probably not the best timing, but I would like to know."

"Sure, what is it?"

"You are so respected by your customers, is that what keeps you motivated?"

Just like as if he were a professional newscaster, he immediately gets right back to the Les Brigham that Jerry knows.

"Jerry, as professionals in this business there is one aspect of ourselves that must be watched, and cared for above all else. It's our attitude. Our attitude is like the wings to our own plane. If it's not structurally sound, our plane is headed for a short flight with a very destructive end."

"I know, seems like attitude is a key factor in motivation." Jerry adds as to keep the conversation focused.

"If our attitude is poor our plane will never get off the ground. If our attitude is healthy, we can perform aerobatics with no concern of failure."

"Motivation and attitude go together like peanut butter and jelly. However it is possible to have a great attitude and not be motivated."

"How does that happen?" Jerry inquires.

"As it has been said so many times from the great motivational speakers, we do most everything in our life to avoid pain and gain pleasure, period. I believe that. I'm not talking just about physical pain, certainly not. There is mental pain and mental pleasure as well."

"We could also open up the topic about goals as well, but I am going to skim over goals in depth right now and address them later. Goals are important, and how we administer them for ourselves is crucial."

Les is on his familiar roll.

"Motivation many times is driven by our self image. We all know who we are, or who we would like to become. If we feel we are off course, much of the time our internal rudder will direct us back on course."

"Keep going," Jerry encourages. He is watching Les's attitude snap back to normal.

"We also have to constantly review how and why we partake in this sales profession. Is it natural? Is it convenient? If not, maybe something else would make you happier."

"You keep mentioning that there may be something else out there as a better fit. Damn it Les, I'm quite comfortable focusing toward this career, honest."

Jerry makes this comment to bring a bit of humor back in and to break Les's spell of intensity. Les can get very focused in his conversation. Jerry likes it when it is more relaxed.

"Shut he hell up, you're going to be fine!" Les says with a big smile. "Back to this motivation thing."

"That's more like it!" Jerry jokes.

"A lot of times we rely on other teammates to keep us motivated. If you are one of the select lucky ones to have a direct manager that helps you with that, you have hit solid gold. Managers many times are reactionary creatures. They get beat on the head from their managers, and before long they create a pathetic message that gets sent out to the sales crew."

"You'll see it in our company at times. I'm trying to work with Dirk when he drifts off down that path."

"I'm going to try and ignore as much of that as I can. I don't think that any type of pathetic rant will do me any good."

"Great idea. If you come up with a system to help you, please let me know." Les responds.

"In reality, there are times when a sales manager will have had very little experience in the field selling, or managing people. This can spell trouble for the sales staff as well."

"It could be a disaster, I would guess." Jerry agrees.

"Yes, just that."

"Back to us again. Bottom line is that you need to determine who you are, what you want, and when you want it, and then design the plan to make it happen."

"Integrity, character as well as ethics come into play here as well. They're all part of the foundation that keeps the structure in tact."

"I'm still listening Les," Jerry throws out.

"Probably the best picture that I can come up with is the overused image of a used car salesman trying to sell a trashed out, worn out car with a new paint job and shiny wheel covers. It gives me shivers just thinking about it. There will be some poor unassuming person listening to everything this man is saying with complete trust as they drive that car home."

"That is questionable ethics right there, I can tell you that." Jerry chimes in.

"You think so Jerry" Les responds.

"Was the salesman unethical in selling the car? No. It is what he does. He sells used cars. If he lied or promised things that were false, then he was unethical as well as dishonest. But we all must remember that a used car is a used car. You get what you buy. Most are sold "as is" meaning no warranty or representations as such."

"Don't make up things the customer wants to hear just to get a sale? Be careful when the road starts leading you down to those tactics. It is a road that lead you right off a cliff. I'm not concerned about you Jerry."

"Thanks Les."

"What about the influence we get from our peers. I realize you are the peer, but what about guys like me? Just starting out? Everyone senior to us could influence our minds."

"Discussion amongst ourselves is like navigating a boat in the river after a storm. You have to be careful for debris, tree limbs, and items the wind has blown in, as well as high water."

"Good analogy Les."

"Thanks, I personally have been lucky enough to find individuals that I can communicate with on a regular basis. We can discuss the activities, the requirements of the job as well as current trends. When either of us have had a success, we tell each other about it. If something has got us twisted up, there is nothing better than having a comrade to listen and make positive suggestions. Don't aggressively search for these people. They will arrive when you're ready for them."

"I know that I have said it before, but you really take this career serious." Jerry says. "If I didn't know better, I would think you owned the company."

Les responds.

"Jerry, every individual that is representing a company must understand that when we are standing in front of someone that knows nothing about our organization, we are the organization. Act like it. Even if the customer is a long tenured customer, they still look to you to make everything easy for them."

"I would agree with that." Jerry adds.

"Perform like you are responsible for everything that happens between your company and theirs. It's also a good idea to look for ways to take on responsibility with your prospective customer and your company. Customers are often mesmerized when they witness a committed, ethical and energetic salesperson. For them it is like watching a good movie. It's a movie that they star in."

"As I am witnessing you and your customers, I take that information to heart. I am watching you prove that at almost every stop."

"It's interesting Les. As I watch you and your customers, a lot of that must get noticed by other salespeople on this team as well." Jerry states in a questioning tone.

"It probably does," Les responds.

"Just for our brief time, I can sense that you have a lot of enthusiasm, but even more you seem to enjoy sharing your thoughts about this career with me." Jerry adds.

He continues.

"You probably are constantly looking for ways to help the other members succeed. I don' know how you couldn't."

"I'm going to take that as a compliment."

"You sure could, it's the truth."

"I think that deciding how much you want to interact and help your team is a matter of choice and it depends entirely on your particular personality."

"OK."

"From reviewing the basics again, our job is to interact and help our customers do business with our company. That is our job as it is defined. We can add a list of other responsibilities, but the bottom line is that we were hired to interact with customers and potential customers resulting in increased business and profit for our company. Period."

Jerry is still nodding.

"Based on that theory, you don't really have to do anything to help your own team. They can follow the 'cookie cutter' outline with some sense of commitment that they are expected to perform routinely, and enjoy a satisfying career."

"I know that there is a 'but' coming along so let me have it." Jerry jokes.

"However," Les holds up his index finger toward the sky as to say 'you are right' here is a question. "Let's use the hole in the road analogy."

"OK." Jerry agrees.

"If you were walking in the back parking lot of our company and you noticed that the pavement had a flaw in it.

You have tripped over that flaw in the concrete a couple of times. You know that your teammates will when they walk in that same area as well."

"OK?"

"Would you want to find a way to get the flaw in the pavement fixed, or just let everyone find it by tripping?"

Les pauses and looks at Jerry.

"After all, you know where it is, and you now walk around it. What else matters? Right? You're safe."

"There isn't a right or wrong answer here, I'm just creating this analogy to make a point." As he says this he is still looking at Jerry in a peculiar fashion.

"Wait a minute, I have to disagree. There's most definitely a correct answer here. It's a safety issue, you must let someone know!" Jerry is showing some emotion about this particular topic.

"I don't care if anyone else trips, why should I? All that matters is that I am safe. Jerry, I'm a business person. I was hired to do a job. I am to go out and secure sales for my company. My job description has nothing in it about communicating with the safety committee."

Les is playing Jerry a bit, but with so much sincerity, Jerry hasn't caught on.

"I don't give a damn about what it says on my job description, this is about being a team member and watching out for the welfare of my fellow dudes."

Les looks at Jerry and just says "Wow!" then he looks forward over the steering wheel.

Jerry is watching Les.

Les starts to form a slight grin and his eyes create a devilish look. Jerry realizes that he has been on a ride.

"Damn it, I fell for it. You were just messing with me weren't you?"

"Yep," is all that came out of Les's mouth. And then a laugh.

"Just for fun though, let's bring it into real life now. Real career."

"Sure."

"Let's imagine you have struggled with a particular step in the stages of processing orders. In your mind, you clearly see a way to readjust a particular step that saves everyone processing orders a substantial amount of time. You have asked questions to key individuals about the process. You clearly and definitely have a fix to help the team. What do you do? Think about this one."

"You have more to say about this, don't you Les?"

"Yep." Les continues.

"Organizations develop systems. Systems or processes that do things. When the system gets understood by everyone, it then becomes habit forming. At that point everyone produces the results using the same routine."

"Everything is fine, right?" Les asks quickly.

"Keep going."

"Innovation can get put on the back burner at that point as everyone just follows the same route. Are there better routes? Does anyone care?"

Jerry looks like he is forming a response when Les keeps talking.

"They say that the way to make a better machine is to ask the person using the machine if there could be any improvements. However, many organizations don't care about that. They just want the machine to do what it has always done."

"Yeah, they call that stagnation." Jerry adds, just to keep the flow going.

"Right, the same is true for you. Can the 'sales machine' that you create be adjusted periodically to benefit you and maybe also your team mates?"

"Remember, we're all on the same boat with the same type of oars. If I can keep my calluses down by holding the oar handle a particular way, I'm sharing it with the guy across the isle. It's just good policy."

"Remember though, as a newbie, many things will be breakthroughs for you, but not for everyone." Les lectures.

"So, do I just keep all of my ideas to myself? Even when I know something can be fixed?" Jerry asks with a strange tone.

"There is a time for everything. All I could say about that is to 'earn your wings' first."

"Many of us veteran sales people know what we do. We understand our processes. Many of us have created our own processes that work well for us."

"It can be satisfying to hear a rookie discover a method that helps them."

"Another 10 miles and we will be at our next call. There's a rest area right up here, should we stop?"

****

Cranston Material Handling was the next call. These folks are tough on Les and he has really never warmed up with them.

"Here we are. CMH as I call them. Interesting folks. Come on, let's go in and see if anything has changed since I was here last month."

Jerry senses some anxiety. "Maybe this will be an account where Les isn't treated like part of the family" he thinks to himself. Jerry wasn't thinking that way as negative toward Les, he just wanted to witness something other than "old home week" when Les walks in.

The two men are met by the receptionist standing out in front smoking a cigarette. Les greets her with a patent, "How you doing," and she just raises her eyebrows as she takes a keep inhale of her cigarette and puffs out a cloud of smoke. She knew she had to go in and officially greet Les and call his contact. She acted as though she had been interrupted during a strategic game of chess.

Les and Jerry stand in front of her desk and wait as she comes in to assume the role of company greeter. She just looks up and stares at Les. Les was expecting nothing more so he asks.

"Is Ron Leland in?"

She picks up the phone and has a short conversation, then hangs up.

"He's busy, did you have an appointment?"

Les has been stopping in here for the last 2 years and the routine is the same. He has made appointments many times and has been stood up. He has even called 5 miles out, several times to confirm, and then upon arrival Ron is too busy. He's really starting to wonder if it is worth it. The income he makes from this company is decent, so it makes it worth his time to stop.

"Well, no I don't. I have been stopping in here every month for the last 2 years calling on Ron. I have made appointments. I've even called just outside of town to confirm and still can't see him. Out of the last 26 stops, I may have had the time to sit down with him 8 times."

Jerry is seeing an unusual frustrated side of Les Brigham for the first time.

"Could I ask you a question?" Les asks the lady.

"What?" she responds with the least amount of enthusiasm she can possibly produce.

"How could I do this better?"

"You can't. He treats everyone the same."

She looks around to see if anyone is watching her conversation and then focuses back on Les.

"I have had people yell at me before, after this same type of episode, as I should be able to go back there and snap my freaking finger and make him change his mind."

Les is seeing a side of this person that is rare, but is also showing a bit of compassion in his eyes toward her.

"I know exactly who you are, and I knew exactly how you were going to get received. It makes me mad every time he does it…..but considering everything in his life….."

Les is sensing something that is not being said.

"What is going on in his life? Can I ask?"

She looks around again. This time she looks over a cubicle wall.

"Sandy, could you spell me for just a quick moment?" Then she whispers something illegible to her.

She walks away from her desk and motions for Les and Jerry to follow.

She is a shapely young lady with a very thin fabric mid length dress. As she gets outside the wind is blowing and her dress is forming many revealing views. Les and Jerry notice this but maintain their professional composure. Jerry, as a single unattached male takes more of an interest. As she gets outside she lights up another cigarette like it was the last one she could have for the rest of her life.

"I'm Jessie, by the way."

Les introduces Jerry.

"Ron Leland has MS. He has had for about 4 years. Eventually it will take him, but right now he is coping. He is in so much pain constantly he really has a rough time focusing."

She looks at Les as though she just gave him the keys to the front door and the combination to the company safe.

"I appreciate the inside information Jessie, I really do."

"We have people come in here all the time and get stood up by Ron. They get so frustrated. But they keep coming back."

"Everyone here is aware of the situation, but most of the vendors are not aware. You have been coming in here for so long, I thought it was only fair that you knew."

"Again, I appreciate that."

"There has been talk about moving him to another position away from seeing people and they may do that in the near future. He is missing more and more work and it is starting to show in his competence, and with our customers. Our fill rate on orders has really taken a hit."

Jessie kept talking, almost appreciative of a listening ear.

"What type of things does Ron like to do, or should I say how does he keep his mind off of the disease? Can I ask that?"

"Sure, his main thing is his grand kids as you have probably noticed from the wall in his office. He is also an avid trout fisherman."

"I have seen all of that. Thanks for reminding me."

"Jessie, its cold out here and you should be inside. Thanks for the update and the inside information. One last question?"

"Sure."

"If I were to send him a card or a note of some type and letting him know I was concerned, would it be received OK?"

"Oh yeah, it would be no problem. It would probably make him feel better as well."

"Thanks again. We'll see you again in the near future. Take care."

As Jessie walks back to her office Jerry keeps his eye on her. The two men get in Les's car.

Les seems frustrated and it shows.

"You seem really bothered. Did you feel you knew him better?"

"No, I really never got a chance to know him at all. He kept me at a distance. I'm frustrated because I should have noticed the signs. It all makes sense now."

"What do you mean, signs?"

"It goes back to normal people skills. At times I seem to forget some basic things when it comes to dealing with people."

"I don't know about that Les, what are you thinking?"

"Normally people are courteous. At least I expect it in people, and I usually see it. I have held animosity toward this guy for years. Ever since he stood me up on my first appointment, and then the second instance, and then the third. I just figured he was a jerk, and I didn't put a lot into my interest. I figured he didn't like me, so why should I care about him. The orders kept coming through consistently regardless. That is a very poor mindset! Very poor!"

"All this time the dude was dying. I didn't even see it."

Les then pulls out his day planner and makes some detailed notes. Jerry doesn't interrupt him while he is writing.

It is now time for lunch and the two find a restaurant and eat.

Chapter Ten

CHAPTER ELEVEN

After lunch they are back on the road.

I want to talk more about this group of people that I will be working with. Can we?"

"Sure, what's on your mind?" Les asks invitingly.

"Well, are they a close knit group?"

"Probably not as much as we could be. We are so diversified as to what we sell, and we all seem to have our specialty niches. Some of our territories are wide and large as well, and other territories are small and condensed."

"What about the personalities Les. Anybody I should watch out for?" Jerry questions.

"No, not as of today. We have had our share of oddities though, I can tell you that."

"Yeah?"

"We have had the new hires that skyrocketed in sales results. Everyone thought that they had the golden touch. Many of the young guys would try to learn from them."

"How'd that work out?" Jerry asks.

"Very seldom will we have a person come in and climb right to the top and then stay."

"Why is that?"

"They are like rabbits. Everything is about closing deals and getting the customer to buy."

"What is wrong with that Les? What if it happens like that for me?"

"Nothing is wrong with generating large sales numbers. Nothing at all. The problems start when the customer doesn't get what is promised to them. Get the customers money and then go find more. And we saw it happen with these guys."

"Is that a salesperson problem, or is it an organizational issue?"

"Good question Jerry. These 'rabbits' as I like to call them are not long term thinkers or providers. It's just about how much money they can earn."

"I'm sure that the management doesn't have an issue with a 'heavy hitter,' do they?

"No, not at all. And don't get me wrong, guys and gals that can produce big numbers ethically are my hero's as well. I think that the issue is in the interpretation of the word ethics."

Les continues.

"You are going to create peers in this organization, as well as develop into one. But choose them wisely. That's all I am saying."

"I understand that Les." Jerry says.

"Sure you do. Don't get caught up in glitz, and a lot of self promotion from an individual. Also, be careful as to being influenced as to what the general audience is saying."

"I am sure there are those out there that are just going to be followers. Aren't there?"

"Sure, an individual could have the whole sales department believing that they are a star performer. And they may be. However remember. Sales standouts, as well as human standouts are not made up of followers, but rather believing in their own integrity and character and acting appropriately. They keep a close watch on their own beliefs and actions and keep that balancing act in check. They don't have to promote themselves, or have anyone do it for them."

"I know that this makes me sound judgmental, but what I am trying to convey here is that just because a person is believed to be a great salesperson, and consistently turns in strong results doesn't mean that you should accept and mirror that individual."

"I have worked with several individuals throughout my sales career and I can tell you that everything out of the 'superstars' mouth is not useable for me. Some have been great people and good friends. Others have been less than credible, but idolized by the management team because they can constantly pull in dollars. Here again, that is what they are being paid to do, but it is important to choose what is being projected."

"I'm sure my better judgment will direct me through it just fine." Jerry states with confidence.

"As I have said before, I'm not worried about you, but just choose your peers wisely, and don't lose focus as to who you are as a person."

"You know Jerry, I'm very confident that you will do OK. However, as I said earlier, time will tell you if this is a profession for you. And time only. It can be very hard at first. Overwhelming."

"I know that it looks great riding along on a trip with someone else, but when you are on your own, things will start to happen."

"Such as?" Jerry asks.

"Starting out you could be pulled in so many directions, by many individuals for many reasons. Your world could start to spin so fast that you may not know which end is up. You may have to look at your driver's license every morning just to remember what your name is. I will guarantee you that your character and personal ethics could get challenged once and a while. Your high points will be 'high' to off the charts, and your lows will be so low you will have to unlace your shoes to get air."

Les is on a roll again.

"You will have days that you feel you have the best job in the world, and wonder why they even still pay you for such experiences. You will also have days that you feel like a complete loser, and wonder if your position is on the chopping block. You will deal with customers that will take you for granted and treat you like a door mat. You will also meet individuals that are kind and genuine people, and will invite you into their personal lives. You will become personal friends. You will have months that money is flowing like it is coming out of a machine. You will also have months that you will wonder if you will even get a paycheck."

"You are really not holding back, are you?"

"No, it wouldn't be fair. You need to hear this stuff. No surprises that way."

"Les, we talked about this earlier, and just a recap. I could have a job that I am not personally involved in. Or I could just be a drone performing a set schedule of routine tasks. I would be able to go home each night from that type of job and turn it off. Or, I could go home every night from that type of job and drink because my career is so mundane."

Les picks up from there nodding his head.

"Just as we mentioned earlier, I personally do not know how you will be successful in a sales position without taking it personal. Taking it personal translates into dealing with emotions. The sales career is built on passion. A real passion. You must be engaged. It shouldn't be boring. Everyday could and should bring a totally new experience. That is the beauty of this career."

"So what do we do when things are going drastically wrong for us, or our customer? It must be emotional. How about getting prodded a bit by our manager when we are struggling in a sales slump? What about not having a good answer for a customer regarding a problem that took place out of your control? I can see the emotional element." Jerry adds.

"We must stay grounded and selectively un-involved. I know that is a contradiction to what I have mentioned about taking it personally and finding ways to do everything for your customer."

"I think I understand it, Les."

"When emotions get involved, we need to create and practice a few simple mind games that relieve the stress and those emotions. It can be done and it is crucial that we learn it early."

"Do you want to hear a story, Jerry? It's a bit lengthy, but you may find it interesting."

"Sure, what am I going to say? No? I'm riding in the car with you. I'm going to hear it anyway." Jerry was having fun with Les, as he punched him lightly in the arm."

"Exactly, you're going to hear it anyway." Les says trying to talk with a huge smirk on his face.

"I remember growing up and having a problem with my car. It was a fairly severe issue and the repair was labor intensive. I knew how to do the repair, but it was going to take some creativity on my part to make it possible."

"Did you need to pull the engine?" Jerry asks.

"Almost. I had to replace a rear main seal. That's an oil seal that keeps the oil in the oil pan and not leaking out around the rear section of the crankshaft. In plain terms, it's one of many parts that keep your car from dripping oil in your driveway."

"I know, I grew up working on cars. This could be a good story."

"Good." Les continues.

"And yes, we are still talking about mind games to avoid stress, and I am heading in that direction so hang in there."

"I'm with you, don't worry." Jerry replies.

"I needed to put the car up on a lift so I could remove the transmission."

"Oh yeah, or under a tree in your back yard with wooden blocks, huh?"

"My friend Mike worked at a local service station. In those days service stations were places that only sold gasoline, and usually had a mechanic on duty. Most all service stations had lifts to lift up cars. The only food you could buy was a stale candy bar out of a beat up old vending machine."

"One night I was telling my friend that I needed to use a lift somewhere, and he suggested I use the lift at the station he worked at. I was hesitant, but he suggested that I do it on a weekend when he was the only one there, and it wouldn't be a problem. Something was still telling me that I shouldn't do it. But, I had to get this leak fixed. Oil leaks are just wrong."

"I agree, I hate oil leaks too."

"So, on a Saturday afternoon I arranged to stop by the station and scope it out."

Jerry interrupts. "I sense trouble coming."

Les looks at Jerry, as to agree.

"My friend was there and he motioned me to run the car in the service bay. He then adjusted the lift points and we put the car in the air. We both walked under the car and looked at its oily underside. It was horrendously messy. I needed to fix it."

"My friend pointed to the tool box in the corner and said to 'get at it.' So I did."

"A customer pulled up to the fuel island and my friend went out to fill up their tank. I was maneuvering the transmission jack into place when I heard a voice."

"What in the hell are you doing?"

"I looked over to see the owner of the station standing there with a very disgusted look in his eyes. I didn't know this man personally, only what he looked like. This was him."

"Oh crap, this can't be good." Jerry interjects.

"I told him that Mike said it was OK to work on it."

"He asked me what I was going to do."

"I told him I was going to pull the transmission and replace the main seal."

"Like hell you are. Get this thing down and out of this bay. I don't have insurance to cover any injuries or damage from a non-employee working on their own car. I'll have a talk with Mike as well."

"I bet you felt a bit uncomfortable."

"Oh yeah, uncomfortable wasn't the exact word for it. I felt like I broke a Federal law."

"Mike didn't lose his job, but at that point I didn't care much if my friend got kicked in the pants or not. I was embarrassed but more disappointed with myself for being in that position to begin with. I was very young and inexperienced, but I knew that this was wrong."

"After the 'smoke' settled and Mike and I were reviewing the experience while driving around town that night he said something quite profound. Remember we were a couple of teenage kids. I was probably oversensitive to things, but he had quite a different perception."

"I was relaying to him how uncomfortable it made me feel to be 'caught' like that doing something that wasn't right and getting yelled at by the owner that didn't even know me."

"Mike just said, 'To hell with him if he can't take a joke!' We both then laughed until we had pop coming out our noses."

"Yeah, he was wrong for permitting me to be there, yet trying to help me out as well. I was wrong for being there, when I consciously knew the rules."

"Were we downplaying and disregarding the owner's rules? Yes. I think that we were dealing with the situation in a matter that didn't hurt us. We kept our friendship strong. His comment made me feel that I didn't get him in trouble, and I didn't feel that he got me in trouble either."

"I think that I get the point, but tell me anyway." Jerry requested.

"The moral to this whole story is that I have used that statement whenever I get in a situation that needs to be lightened up. It helps me put things in perspective."

"I can see how it would do it, and it is a great tip." Jerry says. "What do you do today if you get upside down with a superior or another manager? Even worse, a customer?"

As Jerry was asking these questions he kept realizing that the information that Les was tossing out was actually good information. That fact, and the enthusiasm that Les exhibited made the conversations quite worthwhile.

"Good question, and fortunately I have an answer. This works for me, but it could work for someone else as well."

"Conflicts with another person are quite rare for me. I actually try to avoid them if possible. That is not actually a good trait to have, but unfortunately I am what some may consider 'pro conflict avoidance sensitive.'"

"So, do you get scared of arguing with anybody?" Jerry asks.

"I don't get scared at all. I just don't like to deal with difficult people. However, I really don't think that it is an uncommon trait. I wasn't built with the 'defensive' gene."

"Don't you think also Les, that being a seasoned sales guy, you put a lot of emphasis on positive interaction? I mean after all, isn't that what we are supposed to be good at?"

"That is why I do this, and why I do it well. It's my specialty, and it should be for any successful salesperson out here."

"OK, so again, what do you do when you find yourself upside down? Maybe you screwed up and someone blasted you. Maybe something came up that went a little too personal and it really bothered you. And yes, I'm still talking about personal interaction with another person."

"I actually have a little form that I made for myself. It has questions that I ask myself and I document them honestly."

"What are those questions? And yes, I would love to have a copy of that form, thank you very much!"

Les laughs, "I'll be sure and get you one and you can print it off. Make as many copies as you want."

"The first question that I ask myself is to list 3 ways that the conflict could have been avoided. I give this some serious thought."

"I'm sure."

"Then I ask myself if the situation was entirely a result of my actions, or lack of my actions."

"Next, I decide if this situation was a rare case, or have I been down similar paths in the past. As an example, was this a power struggle, a personal jab at me, or a rumor that I shouldn't have been involved in, etc?"

"Keep in mind Jerry, I document all of this so I can look back at it."

"I get it Les."

"Then I want to document to the best of my recollection, what type of physical reaction did I feel. Cold chills, sweating, shaking, you get the picture. Was I experiencing a lack of sleep over it?"

Jerry nods in agreement.

"Then, it's important that I rank this particular conflict. The question that I ask is, 'Does this qualify for the list of my top life conflicts, why or why not?'"

"And then the final documentation I make on this I ask. 'When am I going to erase this event from my memory?' And I write down a date."

"That sure seems like a lot of work to go through, just because you got all 'twisted up.' How often have you had to go through that exercise?"

"That's the beauty of the exercise. By going through that exercise, it makes me keenly aware of how it happened, and it helps prevent me from doing anything like it again."

"But, how many times?" Jerry persists.

"In the last 5 years maybe 3 times. It really helps in keeping me aligned. I also read some stuff to help me form some positive self talk." Les adds.

"What type of stuff, Bible scripture or something like that?"

"No, but that could work for some individuals as well. I made up my own dialog to think about."

"Examples?" Jerry asks.

"First one. Don't hold post mortems. In my mind that tells me to not dwell on the event. It is in the past. Let it go!"

"OK, what else?"

"I tell myself that thinking about this event hurts my future peace. If I haven't made notes about it and taken steps to prevent this type of event from reoccurring, I need to do it immediately. I need to erase it from my memory so I can add new positive events."

Jerry continues to nod, listening intently.

"Then I tell myself that mostly depressed people keep rehashing the past. I'm not depressed. I'm a thriving, positive human being that sets positive examples for others. I want to continue to be that person."

"And then my favorite one, and you have already heard it. 'To hell with them if they can't take a joke.'"

"I figured that one was coming up eventually. I would have been surprised if it didn't."

Les waits for Jerry to finish, almost as though he was interrupted in mid sentence and then continues.

"I have to tell myself that again that I am a mentally healthy person. Mentally healthy people live, learn, and move on to new positive experiences. Act like a mentally healthy person, because I am."

Jerry is now just watching Les. He can sense that this is a big deal for him to be able to explain his concept.

"Remember, the past does not equal the future. I throw that one in there as well. And yes, here is the last input I go through."

Les is looking at Jerry to see if he is still interested.

"If another person is involved with this issue, and if they are healthy individuals, are they even still thinking about this? If they are still hanging on to this issue after a fair amount of time, it says something about them personally, and be sure and log this into my mind, before I have future conversations with them."

"Wow Les, are you finished?" Jerry asks in a semi joking tone.

"Yes I am thank you very much." Les responds in the same fashion to dilute the intensity that he just went through.

Chapter Eleven

CHAPTER TWELVE

It was time for another stop on the "Jerry Feldman Training Excursion."

Les and Jerry were bonding well. They both seemed to have similar personalities and that surely helped. Jerry was interested and focused. Les enjoyed that. Les in his secret vanity also enjoyed having an audience. Les was extremely confident, as well as at times he was his own biggest fan. Times like this, when he had the opportunity to share his knowledge with others put him over the top.

"Jackson Machine Works, coming up here on the left. That's our next stop." Les announces as though he was a director on a tour bus.

"I think we are going to have a day of unpredictability when it comes to visits Jerry."

"What do you mean by that?"

"This is another sketchy account. I always get to see the folks, but not much fun. Maybe this time it will be different."

"Just remember to smile." Jerry laughs.

"Exactly!" Les shouts back.

They get out of the car and Les opens up the trunk and grabs his hard hat and safety glasses. The ContainPro logo was almost worn completely off from the miles of riding and rolling around in the trunk of Les's car.

"Do I have to have those as well?" Jerry asks.

"We'll get yours at the door. Follow me."

As they enter the building, directly to the left is a shelf and an old bucket. Badges labeled "VISITOR" are lying all around. Hard hats of all types are stacked on the shelf. Some so dirty you could get filthy just looking at them. Jerry sifts through them trying to find the cleanest one.

"Just grab one and put it on! They won't bite you!" Les yells. He had made the comment in such a tone that it appeared he had transformed into someone else.

"Oh blah, blah, blah!" Jerry yells back. "I don't want to look like a coal miner when I walk out of here today. Jerry frowns and smacks him lightly on his hard hat. Les just smiles.

Jerry looks for an unopened pair of individually wrapped disposable safety glasses. He gets lucky and finds a package.

Jerry puts on the hard hat and tries to adjust the head band so it doesn't wobble. He makes a quick adjustment and tries it on for size. It's too loose so he makes another attempt. This time he gets it about right. His hands are now covered with grease and old dust. The hat is positioned on his head in a fashion that makes him feel like a Christmas tree with too big of star stuck on the top. He then puts on his disposable safety glasses and it's apparent to him that clear vision is not what these things were created for.

There is no receptionist here, just an open door on the side of a warehouse configured building and a cleared path through a myriad of different greasy and unassembled projects. The air smelled of cutting oil and stale cigarette smoke. The floor was sticky and littered with crushed pop cans and stomped out cigarette butts. The noise was at time ear piercing.

"Almost forgot!" and Les handed Jerry a pair of disposable ear plugs.

"Ear plugs!" Les yells as he them to Jerry. "Put them in!"

"Thanks!" Jerry yells back.

Jerry knows how to twist the earplugs to get them in his ear. He is thinking to himself as he puts them in place that they were the final touch to render most of his more critical senses useless. He can't see clearly, he can't hear, and if he moves too fast his hard had will fall off and go rolling across the floor. He's in a building with heavy clunking metal presses working, monster sized pieces of steel being transferred overhead. Oh yeah, this is industrial supply selling at its finest.

Once they get deeper in the building Les just looks at Jerry and hand motions him to follow.

Steel presses were stamping out strange designs. Men in greasy uniforms were collecting these items in what looked like personalized wheelbarrows. Some had racing emblems on them, others had racing stripes, and yet others were sporting these bucketed devices adorned with adult oriented graffiti. The men wore large safety glasses and a myriad of different hard hats.

As they followed the sticky path Jerry was enjoying seeing all of the activity. At one instance he stopped just to watch a machine bore a hole in what looked like a four foot thick piece of solid steel. The person running the machine was unusual. A shapely person with strong biceps, but with long hair and what appeared to be female breasts. It took Jerry a moment to figure out that this was a woman, as he wasn't expecting to see a woman operating such an unusual machine.

Les noticed him stopping to look and grabbed him by the arm and pulled him away.

"She's a tough cookie!" Les yells. "One of the best machinists in the state. She has more certificates than I have socks. Un-freaking believable!" Jerry just shakes his head as he follows Les, and hoping that his hard hat won't fall off.

Loud buzzers are going off continually and flashing warning LED lights. With all of the noise and activity, as a visitor you really have to stay focused as to what you are doing. Temperature changes go from hot to cold throughout the path.

Les leads Jerry to a big white thick door smeared with greasy handprints around the handle. Les punches in a code on the keyboard entry and it emits a loud buzz. Les grabs the handle and opens the door.

Once inside and the door closes and it is almost soundless. The men remove their earplugs and hard hats and glasses. It's a little cleaner inside, but not much. Carpet is on the floor, but it was surely a design flaw. It is wrinkled and soiled beyond belief. Holes and stains make it almost unrecognizable as carpet. Cigarette smoke is thick.

Les walks down a narrow hallway and walks in a small office. A radio is turned up unusually loud for a business office playing country music. Johnny Cash singing 'Ring of Fire' playing currently. A man behind a cluttered desk looks up and says "How ya doin?"

Les doesn't recognize him but this was standard procedure for this company. Nothing was ever stable. Les had been calling on this business for almost 2 years with little to show for it. Someday hoping for some stability and someone that he could get to know were all he needed.

"Not bad, how are you?" Les replies.

It doesn't appear Les is real well known here. Not the usual greeting for this seasoned and well liked representative.

"Les Brigham with ContainPro." Les throws out.

"What do you need?" the man says as he takes an empty bottle and puts it up to his mouth and excretes some tobacco juice. He then rearranges the wad in his mouth.

"I really don't 'need' anything. I wanted to be sure and drop off a couple sheets on some special items that we could provide for you."

"Les, was it?" the man questions.

"I'm Zack Chambers. I am taking over the purchasing area replacing Mike who was here earlier."

"Nice to meet you Zack," and Les introduces Jerry.

"Here are……"

Zack interrupts Les.

"Dude, here's the deal. We already have more than enough suppliers coming in here showing their stuff. I really don't need any more. I'll take your lit, but you really don't need to make regular stops. Do you guys have a website?"

"Yes, as a matter of fact we do."

"Do we have to log into it to buy from you?"

"Yes." Les responds, sensing he knows where this is going.

"Leave me with the login information and I will take a look at it when I get time. Other than that, I don't have an awful lot for you. It was nice to meet you." And the man goes back to his music and surfing the internet, as is where Les and Jerry found him when they walked in.

Les gets out his pocket organizer and turns some pages. He writes the username and password on one of the flyers as he reaches across the desk and then hands them back to Zack.

"Thanks Zack, call me if you need me."

Zack raises his hand while still immersed into what ever is on his computer screen.

Les and Jerry walk back out the same way they came in. Only this time Les takes a little more time to point out some of the machinery to Jerry and what it does, as he will get to see plenty like it in his upcoming career.

They drop off the dirty hard hat back on the shelf and walk toward Les's car. Jerry is watching Les expecting him to be bothered by the call. Les is exactly the opposite. In fact he is whistling loudly and starting to do his version of a solo Fox Trot and Tango dance step combination.

Jerry looks at him. "Did I just miss something or did that little country hick inside just dismiss your services?"

"Exactly. That's why I'm dancing."

"So, we are supposed to dance when we lose accounts, or when customers tell us to go take a hike?" Jerry asks with a confused look.

"Oh hell no. Not at all." Les responds.

"What has got you so damned wound up and giddy? I think you owe it to me to tell me. After all, this is a training trip, and there surely must be a lesson attached to this crazy attitude." Jerry is laughing while he is talking.

"This company was never a customer. Not one that I ever wanted anyway. You saw the place. How do you think they paid their bills? Do you think they paid on time?"

"By the looks of that dump, I would bet that they never paid at all."

Les explains.

"Two years of calling on them and not enough revenue to pay for milk at my house. The environment is pathetic, not to mention a possible health hazard. I have been going in there just out of pure instinct. It's actually been more from a pathetic habit. A habit that I should have kicked months ago."

"There comes a time when you really need to analyze your accounts and determine if you can afford to keep calling on them. It's a tough one for us. Especially if we make friends with them. No friends here and I got to get out unscathed. It was a win!"

"When I get back in the office, I will turn this back into a house account and my responsibility to see them again is over."

Les was starting to get on a rant so Jerry just let him go.

"Jerry, a good friend of mine Karl Jensen told me something once that I will never forget."

"What's that Les?"

"The first day I met him, we were making calls together. We were blitzing an area."

"OK, what?" Jerry asks.

"He said to me almost bragging. 'Les, I don't have any bad accounts.' I was shocked, and asked him how he could make that happen."

"What did he say?"

"He told me that he introduced all of his bad accounts to his competitor."

"Oh sure, I don't believe that. I suppose he invited the bad customer and the competitions salesperson on a mutual lunch. Probably paid for it as well and made them hold hands too!" Jerry was going a little overboard, but he deserved the time and had the excuse to comment.

"Oh no, he would just keep suggesting that they call his competitor whenever they had to make collection calls, or was getting harassed about something that was continually uniquely wrong in that customers eyes."

"In other words, he would suggest strongly that someone else could provide a different level of service, putting it eloquently."

"Exactly!"

"I just got out of this 'rat hole' with a clean bill of health! They owe us no money. They just were a waste of time. I never saw the same purchasing person twice. It was just an account that I didn't need on my list. And again, yes, I am happy!"

As the men get into the car Jerry watches Les go through his usual documentation routine.

"We have about another two hours of drive time. What are you thinking so far Jerry? Has it been interesting for you, or just confusing?"

"It's been a lot of 'interesting' with a little 'confusing' thrown in. I have got a topic that we need to discuss."

"Let's crank it up. Like I said, two hours of drive time."

CHAPTER THIRTEEN

As they were getting in the car Les's mind flashed back to the cell phone conversation that he had earlier in Myron's office.

It was a call from one of the attorneys that was working on the legal papers for the change of management with Layman and Son's.

The attorney had asked Les how well he knew Frank Winman. Les responded promptly with the story of all their work together.

He asked Les if he knew of Frank's ill health. Les told the attorney that he knew Frank had some health issues but didn't know exactly what they were. Frank hadn't entered into a lot of discussion with Les about health, but alluded to the fact that he was controlling some of his bad habits and was working on getting back on track. Les then remembered how different Frank had looked when he saw him and just assumed that changing environments with less stress helped him a lot. Frank had confirmed that theory in conversations with Les.

What the attorney then told Les rendered Mr. Brigham speechless.

"Frank Winman is terminally ill. Reports are that he has less than 12 months left." The attorney stated emotionless.

Les didn't know what to say. The attorney advised Les to get together with Frank Winman and uncover all the facts. This was a very big piece of the upcoming events and plans for both parties. There needed to be complete and total disclosure.

Initially hearing that news, Les felt betrayed. But in Les Brigham's true nature, he looked for the reason behind the action, and chose not to go "postal" on Frank until he had a chance to sit down and discuss things.

That morning as Les heard Myron and Jerry coming down the hall he transformed back into his "professional salesman compartmental box" and completed his duties with the customer. He knew he had to stay focused for Jerry as well. He could find things out later that evening.

Jerry again noticed a difference in Les's behavior. It was like he was preoccupied and in another world. He wasn't going to go through the 'intervention' invitation again so he would just get Les back involved in conversation. And he knew how to do it.

"OK, here is the first ball. How do you stay organized? I know that is a general question, but answer it in general terms if you would. I see you use a lot of paper and pen. I've seen others use PDA's and laptops. What do you find best?"

And just like a trained animal, Les snapped right back into his familiar mold.

"Organization is such a key element to success. Not only in sales, but in any type of career."

"Something that I found early was a company called Franklin Covey."

"I've used their stuff too." Jerry states.

"As you know then much of the Franklin Covey material is built around paper and pen technology. Hearing this you probably think that it is obsolete. You are probably thinking paper and pen is a bit outdated. And, yes I am aware of the contact management software out there. I use it as well."

"I was sure you did. There would be no way to share your information with the organization if it was in your own personal paper library."

"I moved away from paper and pen for quite awhile. I was entering the activity information into my PDA or laptop. I was re-arranging my schedule digitally and never scratched out a word or had to erase."

"I don't see you doing that now. What happened?"

"Here is the reality. You will never do away with pen and paper. It won't happen so don't try. You may think that you can do everything on your PDA or your laptop but you will still need to write things on paper. In my opinion it is the fastest method in the field."

"That being said, you can still transfer your handwritten notes into digital form often. It is required by our company to have that type of record. You will learn about the software we use later in your formal training."

"I don't have an issue with computers, so I'm not too concerned." Jerry reassures both Les and himself.

"There's more to the story. I have used many types of contact management programs as well. Using one that I feel confident with or even the one required to use by our organization is a very good thing."

"Every day must be prioritized initially. You must start out with a plan. The most valuable thing that I learned from the Franklin Covey System was that simple 'to-do' lists don't work."

"Why not, mine usually do." Jerry throws out.

"Probably not as good as they could. Anyone can write a few things on a napkin and go after them trying to get each one completed. Only to find out the next day that there was no thought put into the priority of the list. Most individuals will get the easiest ones done first, therefore feeling like they accomplished a lot."

"More quantity than quality is what you are saying?"

"Very true. Franklin Covey emphasizes that each task is either an 'A', or 'B' or 'C.' An 'A' task must be done, the 'B' tasks should be done, and the 'C' tasks could get done. That step alone creates magic. But then we take it one step further. You will most likely have more than one 'A' task. You need to prioritize those tasks by numbers. 'A1,' 'A2,' 'A3' etc. Do the same thing with the 'B' tasks. And then the 'C's.'"

"Start at 'A1' and complete it. Then tackle the next one in line, etc. You may not get through your list. Carry forward the undone tasks to the next day, and prioritize again using the same system. It works. It works very well. If you can't get anything done using this system, you will never get them done using anything else."

"Did you hear the success story about task prioritization?" Les asks Jerry.

"Probably not, what is it?"

"There is a story about a very successful steel company magnate years ago that was struggling with getting things done. He hired a consultant to give him some advice. The man told him to do the following."

"At the beginning or end of each day write down the 6 most important things that you need to get done on a piece of paper. Then number them in their importance. Start off with number one, and don't go after the next one until the first one is completed. It doesn't matter how long it takes. It is the most important and demanding task. Complete it. Then go on to the next. Rumor is that the consultant offered this advice to the man with no expectations of immediate payment. 'Just try it and see how it works' was the consultant's advice."

"And what happened?"

"Weeks later the consultant received a very sizeable sum of money in the mail from his client. A note attached stated that from an efficiency standpoint, it was the best advice he had ever received."

"I think that it is so hard to stay on task as well as being consistent with things like that. It has to take practice."

"They say it takes 21 days of continually doing the same thing over, before it becomes a habit."

"Now, let's take this planning thing one step further." Les asks.

"OK." Jerry responds.

"How many times do we get up in the morning with no real concept of what we are going to do first, or even why we are doing it? Many times we start the day letting the universe have its way with us."

"It happens most of the time to most all of us." Jerry responds.

"Just for the sake of conversation, wouldn't it be awesome if we were able to create a blueprint of what we were to do each and every morning. How we were suppose to think. What type of reactions we 'will' have when certain circumstances come up. Could you imagine how easy it would make our day? What about the stress level?"

"Are you talking about a user's manual to daily living?"

"Sort of I guess. One written by ourselves, about ourselves. Exactly for us. Would that be cool, or what?"

"Imagine that when you encounter a conflict with somebody or something. What is your normal response now?"

"I just get mad, and quite honestly that doesn't get it resolved." Jerry says.

Les volunteers his plan.

"Here is mine. I over think it and stew on it until my brain numbs it out by thinking of other things. Then....I flash back to it from time to time to see if it is still a stressful thought. Oh yes, I am consciously and subconsciously thinking of solutions, even though I say that I flash back to it."

"I kind of do the same thing," Jerry adds.

"If it is a big enough conflict I let it take priority over my conscious thoughts resulting in mistakes in other areas. And this isn't just about interpersonal conflicts. This can happen regarding situations that are totally out of my control."

"And yes, I do use my questionnaire regarding conflicts, but usually not until I realize it is a big conflict."

"I'm getting it."

"What if you were to be able to have an easy to access personal reference library at your fingertips. This reference library would be created in flowchart fashion and easy to use. Here would be a scenario."

"I'm ready." Jerry says.

"You are working on a project. You're very focused. You also are multi-tasking a few other things. All of a sudden the phone rings and one of your customers ask you a question that requires some major effort on your part, and much of the effort is unknown. The typical 'gray area.'"

"I'm with you on this, keep talking."

"You instantly read a few qualifying questions from a list. Depending on the question that most addresses the concern you are then forwarded to another small group of questions. This process repeats itself in a flowchart fashion a couple of more times until you now have your first step determined as to how to address the new priority issue."

"So then we just follow the plan. When things get unclear, just refer to Option 1, Option 2, or Option 3. Is that the concept?"

"It's exactly the concept. It would take some work, but it could be done."

"Sure it could. After you have been in the selling profession a while every thing starts to make more sense. Circumstances that derail you can be categorized into simple and general types. As an example."

"Personality issues. That could be the entry qualifier for Option One. Issues that you encounter while interacting with those around you."

"You've got product and service issues. Option Two. The problems that directly relate to the product and services you are offering.'

"You have administrative issues. Option Three. Problems that directly relate to how the flow of business takes place between you, your company and your customer."

"And you will always have beyond your control issues. These are the problems that you have no control over."

"There are probably many more, but let's keep this simple for now."

"OK, this may turn out to be rewarding, maybe. You've been thinking about this for a while haven't you Les?"

"Oh yeah, for quite a while."

Les continues.

"Let's look at these 'Options' now as neighborhoods that house the particular problems. You have a problem, which neighborhood did it come from, and where does it belong? If we can just get and keep the problem contained in its own neighborhood we are way ahead of the game. Once we are in the right neighborhood, we can then build in some 'navigating' type questions that can help us work through the issue."

"It's very much like programming our minds like a computer to default us to a certain response, depending on the issue. It's intriguing Les, that's for sure."

"Could you imagine what would happen if you could consciously determine and create the outcome of most any given conflict?

"You have probably heard the formula, E x R = O

"The formula of 'Event' multiplied by 'Reaction' (our reaction to the event), will equal the 'Outcome.' Simplified, it is stating that the outcome of any conflict is very much determined by our reaction to the event."

"That makes a lot of sense."

Les flips his turn signal to the right and enters a small warehouse community right off of the Interstate.

"Who's our next victim Les?" Jerry asks.

"It's a new account for me. I just started calling on them this year. They seem to be an organized group of people. They have been very good as far as paying their bills. Easy to work with and so far I haven't had any issues. Let's go see how they are today. And by the way, this will probably be our last stop for the day."

"Cool." Jerry replies. "Where are we staying tonight?"

Les stops like he is frozen for a split second.

"Damn, I forgot to get us rooms for tonight. Well, I really didn't forget, I just should have done it earlier. I'll take care of that right now."

Les hits a speed dial button his cell phone and checks availability in a nearby town. He got lucky for this time of the day.

After a brief conversation he reports, "It's all handled," stated with an expressed undercurrent sigh of relief.

He looks at Jerry with a smirk.

"We're not going to say anything to your wife, are we?" Jerry says remembering the conversation about how Cindy gets on him about getting over involved in his day.

"She only gets whacked at me when I end up staying in a dive motel. She knows I won't sleep well and that concerns her."

Jerry just smiles.

Les directs the car into a parking space a fair distance from the front door of the business.

"Why park so far away, don't you want them to see who you are?"

"It's my personal policy to never take up parking spaces intended for customers. You might keep that in mind as well. I feel that if you take the close spaces up front it sends some mixed messages."

"What kind of messages?" Jerry asks.

"I think that it makes me look lazy. Almost like I need to get as close to the door as possible because I am in poor health or something."

"Really?" Jerry responds.

"Absolutely, and it also says that I have little respect for their customers. If I took the last parking space up front, and one of their customers had to park a distance away it could send a message to the customer that this business is inconvenient to patronize. They could also see me as a person disrespectful toward their business."

"I never would have thought about something like that." Jerry says almost with a guilty tone.

"It's just these little things that you do when you arrive at a business that speaks volumes of who you are."

"I'm getting it. It's right up there with smiling." Jerry includes.

Les nods in agreement.

The two men enter the front door of yet another business. No receptionist here to greet them, just an empty room that looked like it was filled with cubicles at one time. There was a musty smell in the air and the carpet looked like it could use a good cleaning. Some of the fixtures were dusty and general small litter on the floor. It looked like they had fired their cleaning service right after Les's last visit.

Les is looking around like he was there for the first time. He looks at Jerry.

"This is definitely different. Something has happened here, and I'm not sure what." He looks concerned.

A young man is walking toward them from a distant doorway.

He walks up to Les not saying a word but with a look in his eye like, "what are you doing in here?"

Les looks at him and says. "Is this still Hallbarker and Finzer?

The young man looks at Les and says weakly. "Yeah."

"Is Gary Staldman in? I don't have an appointment but he usually sees me without one."

"Gary no longer works here. He was part of the layoffs that took place earlier this month."

"What happened?" Les asks. "The last time I was here this place was booming. Are you guys all OK?"

Les was quite curious as to why all of the changes.

The young man was still emotionless.

"We are in the process of closing the facility," is all he would respond.

"I'm Les Brigham with ContainPro. We have done business in the past and I dealt exclusively with Gary."

Les figured out quickly that the young man he was talking to was just there to help clear out the building. An older gentleman was standing nearby listening to the conversation. He walked over to the men and had a very unhappy look on his face.

"What do you guys need?"

Les tried to at least start a conversation with the man.

Les introduces himself again to this gentleman.

The man extends his hand.

"I'm Chauncey Finzer."

"I'm sorry things took a turn for the worse. Are you going to be OK?"

As he felt Les's sense of sincerity the man's frown went away and his hairline went back in almost a relaxed fashion. A bit of calmness started to show through. Les had a way of portraying such sincere empathy it was almost hypnotic.

"This has been a disaster. My business partner has a warrant on him. Our accountant was his accomplice. As far as this business is concerned, it's over." The man had a sad look in his eye.

"My grandfather started this company in the early 1900's. My dad took it over later and I have been here since I was a teenager. When my dad passed away I was the next in line to run it. A few years back we decided to expand. We were going to take on a complete different, but similar service offering."

Les and Jerry were both listening to the man as he was unloading some very serious trauma.

"I brought in my cousin who had experience in our new directed focus."

The man was starting to have difficulty talking because it was so emotional and they could sense his agitation. Les was feeling uncomfortable and Jerry was starting to get restless.

The man continued.

"It turns out that my brilliant cousin was sleeping with our accountant and the two of them cleaned me out. It was no more, or no less than just that. I was best man at his damn wedding."

"When you start to trust folks is when you have to be very careful. Especially relatives."

"I don't know what to say." Les responds.

"There isn't a lot to say other than 'thanks for the memories' and that's about all."

"Do we owe your company any money?" The man asks.

"No, as a matter of fact I was telling Jerry here that you folks always paid very well."

"We probably didn't do much volume with you guys though did we?"

"No, your purchases were fairly small, but were getting regular and I could see some growth. Believe me I feel so bad for you."

"The small vendors kept getting their money. Two of our suppliers got taken for about a million and a half each. It was such a well planned out scheme I don't think anyone could have seen it coming. It all came to an end quickly. Two of our customers paid on delivery in the amounts totaling almost 6 million dollars. Those funds were redirected and spent immediately. My dear cousin and the trusted accountant are not to be found. I'm the CEO."

"Wow," is all that could be said.

"I trusted, and wasn't paying attention and I only have myself to blame."

Les felt compelled to say something.

"I realize that you and I don't know each other but is there anything that I can do to help you at this point?"

"No, I'm actually OK. This was just business. Personally I'm fine and it was time to retire anyway. I'm 71 years old and it's time to have some fun. Now we can do that."

Les figured that the man was probably wealthy beyond belief and could take the hit financially. He figured the emotional issue for Finzer was watching a family business go away because he fell asleep at the helm.

The men exchanged goodbyes and shook hands.

"Take care."

Les and Jerry walk out to Les's car and get in. Once inside Jerry looks at Les and says. "Yuk, that was a difficult story to hear."

"Yeah, it kind of kicks you in the gut if you let it. What a depressing call. In fact, this has been kind of a depressing day. However, in this business I'm sure you get to take the good with the bad." Jerry says, to let Les know he understands the ups and downs of the business.

"Let's go check in to the hotel, and then go have dinner. I may even have a drink with dinner tonight." Les announces.

"I'm with you buddy." Jerry agrees.

There wasn't much conversation on the drive to the hotel.

Going through that encounter with Chauncey Finzer really made Les start to wonder about he and Cindy's upcoming business plans. Considering that, and knowing that he and Frank Winman need to talk about some very serious things had Les a bit twisted up inside.

Chapter Thirteen

CHAPTER FOURTEEN

Les and Jerry check into the hotel.

"I'll meet you down here in the lobby at 6:30, Les advises Jerry. I have a phone call to make and I'll be ready to eat after that call."

"Sounds good to me Les. I hope everything works out for you on the call." Jerry is sensing some real worry in Les's demeanor. Les just hasn't been on his game this afternoon. Jerry wants to know more, just from a curiosity standpoint but knows it isn't his business to pry into Les's affairs.

Chapter Fourteen

Once in his room, Les calls Cindy.

"Hey girl, how are you?" Les asks.

"Just great. How are you?" Cindy responds.

"Well…I'm not sure at this point." Les states with a very unusual tone.

"What's wrong honey?" Cindy asks.

"I found out this afternoon that Frank is terminally ill. Now I need to call him and find out why he has been keeping that from us. I feel like we have been betrayed."

"Who told you this?" Cindy asked.

"One of our attorneys. He called me today."

"Knowing Frank, I don't think he is attempting anything crooked, or deceitful, he probably just has his affairs in order and was planning on bringing us in the loop when he felt comfortable." Cindy always tried to look at situations in a positive way as well.

"I'm thinking the same thing Cin. Frank has been too sincere with this whole thing. He's probably just waiting for the right time to let us know." Les states in a self re-assuring tone.

Les's cell phone was beeping in another call as he and Cindy were talking. Les looks at his phone.

"Cindy, can I call you back? Frank's calling me."

"Sure, call me back."

"I will." And Les answers the call from Frank.

"Dude, what's happening?" Les throws out at Frank Winman on the other end of the phone.

"No much buddy. Are you with your trainee?" Frank knew of Les's schedule this week.

"No, we just finished up and I'm in my room. I was just talking to Cindy......and Frank interrupted."

"You got a call from Chausler today, and I know that my health was discussed."

"Yeah, that's what Cindy and I were just talking about. You were my next phone call. What's going on?"

"First of all, I'm not dying. At least not in the immediate future. By the way, our legal teams are doing a great job of creating full disclosure."

Les is sensing a comfortable tone in Frank's voice and is feeling some relief by listening to him. Frank continued.

"Yes, I am labeled as terminally ill. Medically and on paper it is stated as 'short term' but my doctor and I both feel that I have a quite a bit of living left."

Les was silent on the other end of the phone and Frank continued to explain.

"Les, this business venture that we are working on is rock solid. I can guarantee you that it will be a wonderful arrangement for you and Cindy. I've known you a long time and I know how you react to certain types of things. If we would have told you about my illness we were concerned that you would have over thought the whole situation and possibly made decisions based on more emotional perceptions. I wanted you to take this on based on logic, not pity."

"I could see that." Les adds.

"I have watched you get so personally and emotionally involved with your customer's lives, I just wanted this to be considered for your benefit, and not mine. That is why I have been so happy about you and Cindy coming in."

"I think I feel better Frank, but I still want to know more."

"And you will. And also for the record Sarah and I sketched out an outline regarding our venture together even before we had dinner together that first night. We talked in detail about when my illness would be disclosed. This reveal today was actually on schedule but I really wanted you to hear it from me instead."

"I understand that," Les comments.

"The way this whole reconnect with us has taken place has been almost cosmic. I was diagnosed with this stuff right before Herb passed away. His death was sudden. It's been tough on Sarah. Putting her dad in the ground and knowing I'm on the bus ride 'out' has been quite a burden. Having this company handed to us along with the other parts of the Herb Layman conglomerate has been a fast and furious chain of events. We have not had time to enjoy anything. When you walked in the door that day it was like that puzzle piece finally got delivered. I can't tell you how much I want this to happen for you guys. You and Cindy deserve it."

The thing that kept Frank and Les together as friends during their working relationship, was the sincerity and honesty both men shared. They watched out for each other, and helped one another consistently. When Les changed employers and moved 2 hours away, he and Frank started to drift apart. It was about the same time that Franks' health started to decline. Frank limited his conversation with Les because of the illness, and Les was trying to get comfortable working for a long time competitor. Those circumstances created a more natural exit scenario for their close friendship.

"And we are looking forward to the future as well. But we still need to know more about your health."

"If you and Cindy are available Saturday morning, let's have a conference call between the four of us. We'll pull all wrinkles out of the carpet then. How does that sound?"

"Perfect. I'll text you tomorrow."

"Hey Les?"

"Yeah."

"Don't get concerned. Keep all this stuff in its proper boxes, OK?"

"Will do buddy, will do."

Les then called Cindy and filled her in. Cindy was still a bit twisted up when the conversation ended, but Les knew things would work out.

As Les and Jerry are eating dinner that night the conversation migrates back to the selling world. Jerry has absolutely no idea as to what Les Brigham is in the process of doing. He has no idea of the myriad of questions and concerns that Les is currently sorting through. And because of the way Les has groomed his emotions, Jerry won't find out on this trip.

"You know Les, I can see how easy it would be to separate the professional sales folks from the non-professional. Watching you do what you do, I don't know why anyone would not want to buy from you."

"I'm not sucking up either dude, but I'm thinking that it's going to be so much easier for me entering into this profession as a 'road warrior' and learning your positive habits?"

"Oh yeah, I hope someone can learn from my experience." Les responds.

"You know Jerry, there a millions of paid salespeople out on the street, and in phone rooms everyday promoting their goods and services for the company that they work for."

"Yes"

"A segment of these individuals consistently struggle everyday because the profession is just one of convenience. It provides a good income for them, and they understand the industry that they work in. Not particularly the 'selling business.' These individuals are really not professional or even efficient as liaisons between company and customer, however they do keep a good line of communication going between themselves and their customer."

"OK."

"Another segment looks at the profession a bit different. They have a plan. They have goals. They have a specific purpose for each and every customer. They are consistently thinking about ways to work closer with the customer and integrate that business with the company that they represent. They are aware of their appearance, their health, their communications, their efficiency, and what they are working toward. These individuals are aware of the trends in the industry that they sell to. They also invest in themselves through taking the time and spending the money on personal development. "

"I can agree with that as well."

"And in general terms, there is yet another group of misfits that don't migrate toward either of the previously mentioned groups. They could be combinations of both, or new recruits in the selling profession."

"I suspect that the question is like you mentioned earlier. Where do you want to fit in? They are all valid. They all exist. However, it will prove beneficial for you to determine early the picture you have in your mind about who you want to be."

Out of nowhere Les asks Jerry what appears to be an odd question.

"Jerry, do you ever really think on purpose?"

Jerry had spent enough time with Les that he didn't take offense to the question. He knew that there was more to follow, so he responded directly.

"What do you mean?" He asked back.

"I mean sitting down just for the exact purpose to find answers. Do you ever do that?"

"Is this like brainstorming or something?"

"Yes, it's exactly like that, but I'll bet if you tell me you do it, you don't do it effectively."

"You mean that there is a technique involved? I can't wait to hear this one." Jerry says in a comical way.

"Yes, as a matter of fact there is, and it pays rich rewards if done properly." Les continues.

"It's time to think. How many times have you heard that?"

"Many times," Jerry responds.

"Thinking. It's kind of like exercising except less sweaty. Many times it is not easy. It takes effort."

"Especially when you are tired." Jerry throws out.

"What does thinking consist of? You would interpret thinking as coming up with answers when there are no answers."

"Probably"

"Let's keep this simple, OK?"

Jerry nods.

"Issues and challenges come up every day. We let them bounce off of us like water on a ducks back. Some issues we keep regurgitating in our minds because it makes our conscious mind feel like we are trying. Usually we aren't solving anything. We are just letting it weigh on our minds while we deal with other circumstances. We can label it 'thinking', or we can say, 'we have put great thought into this.'"

This is one of Les's favorite topics. If an airplane lands on this restaurant and wipes most of it away, Les will most likely still be orating on this topic as he is getting loaded into the ambulance.

"Most every second of most every day our mind is constantly scanning ideas and questions. Jumping from one topic, one concern, one thought to another. This happens so fast that we consciously don't even realize what is taking place. It doesn't matter if we are mentally at peace, or in a myriad of turmoil. Without consciously focusing on something exclusively how could you find answers? If you find this hard to accept feel free to test it your self."

"How do I do that?" Jerry asks cautiously.

"Sit still in one place and don't think about anything. Maybe try to concentrate on your breathing. Just be aware of your breathing and nothing else. Don't count your breaths. That requires thinking. Just be aware that you are breathing. Try it tonight right before you get into bed, or even better, after you turn off the lights."

"So, I could do it anytime. Morning, night, it doesn't matter?"

"Sure, go ahead and set your alarm clock for the middle of night, and get up and try it. You're sleeping. You shouldn't have much thinking going on then, huh?"

"I know what your results will be." Les adds. "Thoughts will still be entering into your conscious mind. It's really tough to shut them off."

"You're probably thinking that I am trying to introduce you to the concept of meditation?"

"It sounds like it."

"What I am trying to introduce you to is the concept of real and effective thinking. Very focused and conscious thinking. It is an amazing technique, and it is so simple that it is almost scary."

"Do you want to hear more about this Jerry, or am I boring you on this topic?" Les asks.

"At first I wasn't sure, but I'm getting intrigued, keep going."

"By the way Les, you can tell when I'm bored."

"How?" Les feels he needs to respond.

"My eyes will be closed." Jerry remarks with a smirk.

"OK then I'll continue."

"It's best to find a quiet place free of distractions."

"Let's imagine that you are working on a project. In order accomplish that project you need to create ideas that will help solve a problem. As an example let's use the idea of a more efficient canvassing technique. You need to come up with a better technique for finding and qualifying prospects."

"Great, we'll keep it on our topic of the week. Sales."

"Exactly, what else is there to talk about?"

"It all starts by asking a question. Just a simple question. However, you must put a bit of thought into the question."

"You could ask the question to your self, "How can I find more customers?" Not a real bad question, but we should be more specific. The question should be focused."

"In what way," Jerry asks.

"How about this question instead? What methods could I start to use each day to locate at least 3 new prospective customers?"

"I like it better, I can see that." Jerry remarks.

"Write that question at the top of a lined tablet, or on a blank Word document on your computer. Then write a #1 right below it."

"Now read the question again."

"Then write down the first thing that comes to mind. The very first thing that comes to mind. Don't qualify it, or think it through, just write down the answer that pops into your head."

"Even if it is ridiculous?" Jerry questions.

"Exactly, the crazier the better."

"Read the question again. Write down the second answer that pops into your head. If a thought enters your head, write it down no matter how bizarre it may sound."

"I have heard of brainstorming before, but never like this. I have done it in groups before and if it wasn't a possible solution, the group facilitator wouldn't accept it."

"And that stopped the group from thinking. It always does. You're all in competition at that point to outdo the previous idea."

"That's what usually happened." Jerry says.

"Do you have any idea how many great business concepts came from some wacky idea that no one was brave enough to explore?" Les questions.

"Tons of them, probably."

"To get back on track, here is what will happen when you are doing this on your own."

"You will come up with 5 or 6 answers to your question immediately. Keep reading the question."

"Then, another answer will flow in. Write it down."

Les pauses, looking at Jerry.

"You will probably experience a brief time that nothing will enter your mind. You will also tend to get distracted. Don't!"

"OK."

"Read the question again. And then again. Read that question like it is the most important thing that you have to read that day!"

"Then like magic another answer will pop into your head. Read the question again, and most likely a couple more answers will enter into your mind."

"I must tell you that this may sound easy, but starting out it is anything but easy. Again, it can truly be compared to exercising."

"I'm not sure I could ever focus that long Les. My mind wonders too much."

"Oh I know that much too well."

"Your biggest enemy in using this 'thinking' concept is distractions. Keeping yourself from getting distracted is like trying to start a fire using wet paper. It will be tough."

"Remember, don't spend any conscious effort trying to qualify your answers to the questions. If it pops into your head, write it down."

"Would you like a challenge Jerry?"

"Maybe, what is it?"

"Try this every day for 3 days. Use a new question each day. Try to set aside one hour each day for doing this."

"OK, then what?"

"After you complete your three sessions go back and look at your material. Find the top 3 answers to each question and implement them. Test them. See how it works. Then ask yourself these questions."

"More questions, oh no!" Jerry is adding a bit of levity to the conversation, as Les get rather intense when he is on point about something important to him."

Les smirks, and then inhales.

"Do any of the salespeople or companies that you compete against every day use any type of dedicated, focused thought process to help them promote and sell their products and services? Do they put this much thought into what they do?"

"This sounds much too simple to be very effective. However, I can see how it would work. I can also see how it could help me change a lot of things in my life, as well as succeed in many areas. I will definitely try it, I promise you that!"

"Please Jerry, let me know how it works for you. I tell a lot of people about this, and I know that so few actually try it. I'd like to hear a success story so I feel like my thoughts are valid."

"Hey, Les?"

"Yeah."

"I can't tell you enough how beneficial this time with you has been. I realize that it may be getting boring for you to keep talking about this sales stuff, but it really helps me and I am learning a lot. Thank you again for everything you are doing for me."

"Jerry, it is truly fun. Especially when I am working with someone like you that is intelligent and is taking an interest. You are welcome my friend."

The two men finish their meal and drive back to the hotel and relax the rest of the night.

Chapter Fourteen

CHAPTER FIFTEEN

It's another beautiful spring morning. Les's car is covered in dew from the evening air. He gets out his window squeegee and clears the windows. Jerry witnesses Les clearing off his car windows in the same fashion that an artist puts paint on a canvas. Not a square inch of glass left un-wiped.

"Now I've seen it all," Jerry comments.

"What?"

"You're cleaning your car windows the first thing in the morning. Do you expect me to do this too?" Jerry asks laughing.

Les responds like he doesn't get the joke.

"Well, only if you want to see where you are going. I have found that vision is a big aid to driving a car. However, you could wait until mid morning and let the sun dry it off. But that's probably not the best plan for a productive day."

"I've just never seen anyone do that before, that's all." Jerry responds.

"Funny you should say that. I don't see anyone do it either. But I do see a lot of cars driving around early in the morning with wet windows. I don't know how they see."

"They probably don't until they hit something."

"Exactly."

"I'm ready for my last day of fun and games in the world of Les Brigham?" Jerry tells Les as he gets in his car.

"I'm sure you are," Les responds.

As Les and Jerry head out to visit the next customer Jerry is again reviewing his notes and flipping pages like he is reading a road map.

"Hey Les, how do you deal with the family side of your life and this business? I can see how they could blend together quite easily."

"You kind of have to know how to separate the two. As professional salespeople we are designed and groomed to do a job. That job is to find and create and maintain solid customers. It can get to be very addicting and self consuming."

"I'm seeing that, and thus why I am asking the question."

"As a professional salesperson you will develop a unique mindset. You will turn it on in the morning, and hopefully be able to turn it off when appropriate. And I mean hopefully. Let me explain."

"Please do."

"What I am about to say may sound a bit pathetic to hear and make me sound phony, but hopefully it will make some sense."

"I'm listening."

"Considering all of the discussion so far about sincerity, integrity, character, and honesty this may appear to be a contradiction."

"Let's hear it, come on." Jerry is prodding.

"We as salespeople still 'act.' We are 'on stage' from the time we greet a customer to the time we leave their presence. This procedure takes energy. Early in your career it will tire you out. You will be running on adrenalin most of your early career, excited, interested, focused and exploring."

"OK," Jerry nods.

"As you get familiar with the sales process and your personal routine it will all become too familiar. It is then when the acting and performing will start to take place."

"I am going to be and actor, right on! I knew this would get me somewhere!" Jerry is laughing and looking at Les.

Les looks at him like he has lost it, and keeps going.

"It is human nature to adapt. We as humans are the best adapting creatures on the planet. As salespeople we take adapting to advanced levels. And yes, using those acquired acting skills helps."

Les keeps talking.

"When I travel out of town it is quite normal to be invited to someone's home for dinner. I even get invited to stay at their house. I avoid this like the plague. The dinner thing is tolerable, but the staying at the house is something I will never do. And here is why."

"These invitations usually happen when I am a long distance from home. That means I am constantly interacting with people as my call routine is a bit more condensed. I'm usually taking someone to lunch, and spending much more time in front of customers."

"You actually get wore out, don't you?"

"Yes," Les nods.

"I need the solitude of a hotel room to relax. I need to turn off the 'stage time' that takes place during the interaction with customers. I can not sleep in someone else's home. I'm still 'on.' You may be able to accept the sleepover invitations and still feel refreshed the next morning. It probably has a lot to do with personality types."

"I think I can understand that Les. What about the personal side with your family?"

"And yes, as for the personal time with your family. This is a bit easier."

"Do you really think so?" Jerry responds.

"Sure. Home is your comfort zone. You have your loved ones, your familiar bed, and all the things that make up your personal life."

"OK."

"Your own family is usually quite forgiving. They understand you and love you. You may at times take that for granted in regards to your job as well."

"How?"

"I'll explain."

"Let's say you get up on a Saturday morning and announce that you are up against a deadline this week and you really need a couple hours to get some documents processed."

"That sounds harmless enough."

"It sure is. Your family sympathizes with you and you take care of business. Easy. Right?"

"Your mind then thinks, 'I got it handled, and my family didn't care. That's great.'"

"I'm with you." Jerry reassures Les.

"Then here's another scenario. You're home at night and you wonder over to your desk and start to look at some sales reports. By the time you finish, an hour and a half has passed."

"These types of scenarios will develop into a routine if you don't get a handle on it. Your work life will slowly filter into your private time with your family. Be careful!"

"So what do you do?"

"That's a fair question."

"You plan each day, week and month. You set boundaries as to when you open up your business life and when you close down each day. You set the rules, and you live by them."

"Unfortunately, our jobs as sales people don't start and stop on an hourly basis. It is so easy for your sales career to blend right into your personal life."

"It must be a real conflict with you, especially the way you work so close with your good customers. Customers, versus family. Wow."

"Well, I certainly understand my family. I have that going in the right direction. And they understand me as well, so the arrangement is very good. I know a lot of other sales guys out there that are constantly getting leaned on by their spouse for not being home enough. Fortunately this is my career and my family understands it. I am lucky."

"I haven't met your family, but I can see how you would be lucky if they understand you and your business relationships."

"They are absolutely great!"

"Les, I feel like our time is drawing to a rapid close and I want to re-visit your concept on customer service and helping one more time. I know that it is something you have engrained into your soul, and I think it's important for me to hear again."

"I have no problem with talking about this again because I think that it is crucial to long term success. My obligation to my customer is to help them. Period. We can define help in many ways, but my guiding focus is on helping."

"So Les, is selling them something actually helping them?"

"Absolutely, maybe." Les responds with one eye a bit distorted.

"Why maybe?"

"Anyone can gnaw and work on a prospect until they buy something. That is almost always possible. I try to keep my customers best interest in mind at all times. This can be difficult at times when we are getting strong messages to get products and services sold to hit a particular goal."

"And, I will also promise you that even if you are the most dedicated and helpful salesperson in the world, there will be times when you will sell something that was not the right fit for your customer, but they bought it anyway. And you were very glad to have sold it. It will happen, and it may happen often, especially in tough economic times."

"The purpose of the 'helping' mindset is to create an image for your self. An image that your customer sees every time that they see you. It will make a difference. You will have prospective customers and current customers that will care little about what you personally are trying to accomplish. They will only look at you as a vessel to get the product or service that your company offers. You can help, and wish to help until you turn blue, and it will not register in their mind. You are 'just' the person that they 'must' use to get it."

"Is it that impersonal?"

"At times, yes. You learn to deal with it."

"And to these customers you should still provide your personal service the best you possibly can."

"Even if they seem to be antagonistic?"

"Especially then, but only for a while. If you sense you are truly getting taken advantage of, and your company is losing money dealing with them, use my friend Karl's advice and introduce them to your competitor. But, service them well up to that point."

"You'll understand this customer for who they are, and what they want, but service them well until they are gone."

"I get it. Create the everyday mindset. Create the habit."

"Exactly, and here is why. You will develop into that person. People will know you for the helping person. People will talk about you as the helping person. People will recommend you. People will seek you out."

"So, if I am building up this image of being the helping person but don't really feel it, is it wrong?"

"It depends. What do you call wrong? The correct mindset is critical for success in any endeavor or job."

"Some occupations it doesn't seem like it would matter." Jerry questions.

"Like what, give me an example. Pick any profession."

"OK, as an example, a truck driver. Any type, delivery person, or interstate long hauler."

"Perfect. First of all do you think that all of these individuals love what they do?"

"Probably not all of them."

"That's right. The ones that hated it either crashed, or moved on to other jobs. Those veteran drivers know the same thing. They understand that if they don't help in some way, they will either get replaced by someone that will, or their job will be miserable and much shorter term. They also must help 'their' customer. By their conscientious help they are not only creating an image for themselves, but creating a true positive image for the company they work for."

"We are all selling everyday. But if you break it down to its simplest form we are helping much more."

"OK then, administration people. How do they sell? What do they sell? How do they succeed?" Jerry was asking repetitively.

"Interesting example. Here is my spin. They sell their help. If they are known as a good employee they have helped someone or some department well. They have tried hard. They have sold themselves as performers and individuals that can help and make a difference and get a task done. Were they phony? No. They had a job to do and they knew what to do to get it done and they did it."

"It all revolves around helping, but it gets multiplied dramatically in the sales profession."

"Well then, how do you know who the right person is to service?" Jerry asks because he likes to see Les explain these things with so much passion.

"As salespeople who make calls on prospects and organizations the crucial key is to interact with the person that can get you the money for your goods or services. This statement sounds shallow I realize but it makes sense. It also may sound as though it is a contradiction to what we just talked about regarding helping."

"Yeah, it sort of does, but I know there is a pattern here. Go for it." Jerry encourages.

"As we perform our jobs as salespeople we will make friends with our customers. It is going to happen. It needs to happen. However for our success and to acquire the ability to sell anything you will need to know who the person is that signs the checks or directs that person to do it."

"So the money person is important? I have to know the Accounts Payable person as well?"

"Maybe not directly, but you need to know someone that can direct the AP person to write your company a check."

"If you don't achieve that task, you are just visiting. Visiting does little good for your success if that is only as far as it goes. It wastes your time."

"So, what you are saying then that strictly from a sales performance standpoint, if I have created a relationship with a person in an organization that has no influence to a buyer, I am wasting my time?" Jerry asks in a curious tone.

"From a sales performance standpoint yes. It's counterproductive. Remember the goal. Provide help to individuals that your services or products help. You only have so many hours in a day to accomplish that."

"OK, now I am confused. I am talking to people that use our products or services. I'm getting to know them. I can help them if they use our offerings. What in the equation am I missing?"

"Remember. You sell, they buy. If they can't buy, you are visiting. Visiting doesn't earn you a commission, as it has not reduced any of your company's inventories by visiting with your friend."

"So it's a bad thing to make friends?" Jerry is trying to be comical now.

"Not for you, it would be a major event!" Les laughs and punches Jerry in the arm.

Chapter Fifteen

CHAPTER SIXTEEN

"Hey Les, how would you define success in this occupation?"

"That's a really good question Jerry.

"When you are reviewing your performance, and or reviewing your occupation I think that it is imperative that you think about how you define success."

"For many in this occupation it is purely based on money or income. Maybe you can base it on a quota percentage. The company that you work for will probably define your success based on a quota percentage."

"That quota thing freaks me out. It sounds so critical. Almost like belonging to an elite club." Jerry says.

"Oh yeah, it can be like that as well if you get all wrapped up in it.."

"To begin with, I feel that first you must understand why you are involved in this occupation. If you sit down and list all of the positives, and then list all of the negatives, which ones are greater?"

"If the negatives are greater am I sunk?"

"No, not sunk. But you should really work on coming up with some more positives, or you may have a tough hill to climb."

"OK."

"Our company will define your success you can be assured of that. Remember, you are performing by their rules, and jumping through their hoops. I don't make that comment negatively toward our organization. They have their agenda, and their developed benchmarks, and that is the way it should be. However, your personal success should be based on your own prerequisites."

"Such as?"

Les starts to recite his list with such emotion and fervor Jerry can tell he thinks about it often.

"Is your job interesting, and does it hold your attention?"

"Do you feel that you are making a difference somewhere or for someone?"

"Do you enjoy the challenges?"

"Can you tolerate the downsides without allowing them to knock you out?"

"Do you get up in the morning enthusiastic?"

"Is your income allowing you the lifestyle you enjoy?"

"Do you feel good about what you do?"

"Are you contributing to the betterment of your team?"

"These are just a few questions that you could ask yourself."

"Those are good questions, I like them.

"You'll know if it is a good fit or not and if you are successful. It's no magic formula. In most people, if they enjoy what they do, they will be good at it. Career enjoyment is one of the leading factors in an individual's success."

"Speaking of 'individuals.' Give me some insight about dealing with personalities." Jerry requests.

"One of the things that you will always have is challenges dealing with people. Not necessarily your customers, but now I'm talking about your own team. Either your teammates or your managers."

"I think that the thing that we always lose sight of is that everyone is different. Every person alive is unique in some way, and lived a totally different life filled with unique circumstances. These circumstances shape our personalities. These circumstances have shaped the personalities of your team mates, and your managers. No one thinks exactly alike, no matter how much we want them to."

"The people that we gravitate toward though, will have very similar interests and beliefs as ours. This is why we gravitate toward them. It's easy, and comfortable."

"That being said, you will have team mates and managers that you have nothing in common with. Plan on it. Your conversations will be a struggle when 'off topic' from your job. It doesn't make any of us wrong. It keeps us human. Our stress occurs when we feel that everyone should think exactly like we do. If we lose flexibility with this fact we harm ourselves."

"I understand that concept. Talking about thoughts, etc, do you think it is safe to share my goals and ideas with my manager?" Jerry asks sincerely.

"I think that your goals and ideas should be shared with your boss. However, only if your boss shows the ability to understand your mindset and can work with you toward achieving your goals."

"And only if that can take place." Les emphasizes.

"Just because this person is your boss, and you have shared your goals and ideals, doesn't mean that your boss can understand and work with you. And, just because this person is your boss doesn't mean that they should be your mentor or confidant."

"You sound as though you are 'down' on management. Do you have an attitude about bosses?"

"Oh heck no. Not at all. However there seems to be an upswing in management style today that is very self centered. This is just an observation, and I have no proof that is an epidemic. It may stem from the business practice that business is just a game of numbers."

"But Les, business is just numbers. Sales numbers, quota numbers, and requirements."

"Believe me, I understand that business is a numbers concept. Successful businesses know how much money they should create to grow. Successful business also put together well thought out plans on how to achieve them."

"So what's the problem?" Jerry asks again.

"The problem can be that, numbers are not people, and sometimes the human aspect is forgotten."

"That is the truth, isn't it? The human aspect of business gets overlooked and companies lose good people based on numbers." Jerry acknowledges.

"Yes, unfortunately, it's true."

"Then, what do you think the role of a manager is? And specifically, a Sales Manager?" Jerry asks.

"I honestly feel that the Sales Manager should be the sales team's biggest cheerleader. I think that they should be on a constant search for positive things happening amongst their group, as well as being keenly aware of individuals that may need help. Communication with every individual in their team is critical as well. We all get beat up out on the streets. 'Our service is poor,' 'prices are too high,' 'quality is questionable' and on it goes. We hear that as salespeople and after a while feel like the complaints are valid. The last thing we need is to return to our office and have a Sales Manager ready to pounce for some unrelated obscure reason."

"Don't you think that the Sales Manager would want to 'shore you up' from the beatings that you may get out on the street?" Jerry comments.

"It would be a great place to start, that's for certain."

"I can understand your opinion Les, but how exactly could a Sales Manager help the team move forward? In a sales slump, for instance?

"As we talked earlier, a salesperson in a sales slump better be communicating with their boss already. They should make it a team effort between them to explore and experiment with concepts to produce results. Unfortunately the message that gets sent to a struggling individual is one of threatening and demanding. Personally, I don't take kindly to threats."

"I don't either and I hope Dirk isn't that way. But I can see him coming 'un-sprung' once in a while." Jerry states in a questionable tone.

"He's working on it. He really is. He and I have had more than one discussion about that precise topic. His problem is that he worries too much about what may happen to him from his bosses, and at times can't interpret it, and relay it to us in a less volatile fashion. I'm seeing big improvements weekly though."

"Good," Jerry says a little relieved.

"What he needs to do is run his own game. I realize that in the corporate world they expect you to act like they do, and preach the same sermon. But Dirk has earned a lot more respect from us when he was his own person and sitting beside us. Earlier on he would come in all pumped up with fire in his eyes and try to intimidate us to action. You can probably guess how that worked out for him?"

"I'm guessing not too well." Jerry answers.

"We had guys walk out of the conference room and out the front door, never to return. And these were good guys too."

"That's too bad Les. I would probably do the same thing, except I'm probably not tough enough to do it."

"I've had my opportunities to do the same thing, but I chickened out as well." Les says in a reassuring tone.

"It's probably more of a maturity thing, don't you think?" Jerry questions.

"We can say that. I like that theory." Les grins.

"Our one and only call today is up here on the right. Do you see that big building?"

"Yeah I do. Is this another one of your personal friends?" Jerry asks with that grin that Les is getting familiar with seeing.

"Not really. I'm just getting to know them. We have some things that they can use. I just need the time to get them to buy from me and not my competitor."

Chapter Sixteen

Les greets the receptionist.

"I'm Les Brigham and I'm here to see Gerdine McCaffrey. I have an appointment at 9."

"Les, let me see if she is available."

"Thank you."

"She is available, and said to come on over." The receptionist advises.

"Thank you very much. We're on our way. It was nice to see you again."

"How is Mr. Brigham today?" asks Gerdine McCaffrey, a very attractive young lady that is VP of Procurement.

"I am absolutely phenomenal, how is your world?"

"It just can't get any better Les," she replies with a great big smile and a cute giggle.

"You are always so happy. I love calling on you." Les adds.

"You're so kind."

Les introduces Jerry and the three enjoy a few minutes of small talk.

"So, what's new in the world of ContainPro?"

"Gerdine, you know we always have something new and different to share and I've got them right here. But I came armed today with a couple more new questions for you."

"Ask away Les." Gerdine responds.

"Gerdine, how many TY-896's do you go through in a month?" Les just gets right to the point. He has a look on his face as though he knows something extraordinary and is about to share it with Gerdine.

Gerdine turns back and punches some keys on her computer, and then turns back.

"Last month we went through 6 boxes. 125 to a box, that's about 750."

"Do you know who makes those?" Les asks, knowing the answer.

"No I don't Les, who?" Gerdine asks innocently.

"We do. We make almost all of them that are used in the industry. Unfortunately we have a non compete clause with our distribution channels that we have to quote the same price most everyone pays on the street. What that means is that I can't come in here and undercut Campmore, who I assume is your current supplier."

"So where are you going with this Les?" Gerdine asks with that patent cute wide smile.

"We are one of the largest manufacturers and distributors of industrial supplies nationwide. I'm not saying that to brag, or to sound arrogant."

"OK?" Gerdine is still not sure where he is headed.

"You and I have gone over our credit policy many times. As you know on single tier pricing we can offer dating. On some items we also offer consignment arrangements. I restock your shelf, and you only pay for what you use."

"Keep going, I know you are headed somewhere."

"Could I make an appointment with you on my next trip up here to go through some of your inventory? I'd like to see if I could provide some type of benefit for purchasing some items from us?"

"Les, I currently use mostly 3 vendors. You are 4th on the list. Our relationship is new and I'm confident that you will move up a level in the future. I just don't know what I could give you."

"I totally understand, and I respect your loyalty to your current suppliers. I realize that my comment sounds rather 'boilerplate' but it really means a lot to hear you say that."

Gerdine nods her head in agreement.

"Gerdine, I personally don't consider it a 'war' out there between suppliers. I try to think that it is, or should be about service and beneficial strategies for working together with my customer. That's my passion as a representative for ContainPro."

Gerdine is nodding her head acknowledging every word that is coming out of Les's mouth. It's that talent he has for being sincere and empathetic based on honest and ethical actions. He exudes it.

Jerry is listening in wonder of how Les comes up with this stuff. Jerry Feldman is strongly convinced that he has found himself a very good mentor.

Les keeps going as he senses that Gerdine is showing signs of listening intently.

"Gerdine, you probably procure about 450 SKU's on a monthly average. Am I close?"

"I don't really know, but you're probably not far off."

"We have a delivery schedule that I know surpasses any of your current providers. I'm sure that you have to keep higher inventory levels on some items based on limited delivery options. Am I correct?"

"Yeah, I stock up on some stuff because I can only order it once a month."

"Would you consider sitting down with me next trip up here and tentatively allowing us to provide 5 or 10 items that we can prove our value?"

Les adds one more question.

"Could I have the opportunity to back up my motives and claims? 90 days with 5 to 10 SKU's and at the end we can review and I'll walk away peacefully if we fail. Also, if we fail on anything, I will promise you we will provide some aspect of our arrangement that will dwarf any minor hiccup that would occur. I'll even put that all in writing, and signed by our General Manager if needed."

Gerdine has moxie and she is about to show it.

"OK Les, what day are you coming up next month?"

"The tenth, just like this month and all the months prior." Les replies.

"I'm going to think about this. It won't be a big deal for me to grant your request. My past has proven that when claims like yours are tossed out, very seldom do they come to fruition. I'll work on a list for you by then. When you come in next month we can go over the list and see if you still have the confidence you are exuding here today."

"Perfect. I'm looking forward to our meeting next month."

"Me too, Les," as Gerdine smiles.

The two men leave and Les is feeling fairly smug. He feels that he has done his job successfully.

As they get into Les's car, Jerry just sighs and says, "You have certainly been doing this a long time. It really shows."

"How's that?" Les asks.

"Gerdine and I were listening to you like we were in church listening to the appropriate sermon."

"Jerry, it again is just about understanding what you can provide, and being honest and sincere. You may find this hard to believe but I am not thinking about commissions when I am in that zone. Money has nothing to do with it in my mind except from a value standpoint in the customer's eyes. I'm glad it shows."

"You do good sir, you certainly do good!"

"Thanks."

After an episode like that Les's mind temporarily snaps back to the events that are being laid out for his future. He's wondering if he will get the opportunity to use the skill set in his toolbox within the world of Layman and Sons. He enjoys this type of interaction with customers. He will surely miss it if he can't exercise it once in a while.

"Well Jerry that was our last call on this trip. Now for the grueling drive back. Let's put about two hours of road behind us and then we'll stop for lunch."

"Sounds good to me," Jerry replies. "Are we going to stop by and see Rudy again? I'm still thinking about those sweet rolls."

"Oh heck yes. That stop will be right on schedule for our mid afternoon snack. You need to meet Luna."

Les is pulling out of the parking lot and Jerry has his note pad out and checking off topics completed as he and Les discuss them.

Les is watching Jerry shuffle his notes and is sensing his organization skills will play a big part in his future success once he hits the street.

"I've got more questions." Jerry states.

"I know you do. I'm watching your checklist get filled, but I see some topics on that paper that I know we still need to talk about. Go for it man."

"What about cold calling Les? What is the big fear about making unplanned calls?"

"Well, the name of the process, first of all."

"Cold calling. Does that sound spooky or what? It sounds cold. Let's look at that topic in a bit of detail. It's actually one of my favorites." Les states smugly.

"Great, I'd like to get your insightful twist on it."

"What is cold calling?" Les asks, and then continues as usual before Jerry answers.

"It's just making an unscheduled stop or phone call to a business that does not know you are calling or stopping by."

"So far the definition makes sense."

"Considering the process and effort it takes normally to make an appointment, a cold call is purely a shot in the dark as to being able to see anyone of interest, or to be able to explain why you are there."

"So are you saying that cold calling is done out of a sign of laziness?" Jerry questions innocently.

"No, not at all. I look at it as a sign of professional assertiveness trying to meet more people."

"Then why do I hear about so many salespeople that fear cold calling so much?"

"I don't know, as I think that it is one of the least stressful activities you can perform, and probably one of the most basic ways to grow your business."

"Really?"

"Absolutely. I would guess that the reason it is so disliked, is because it appears that you are wasting your time. After all, the chances of walking into a business and believing that you will walk away with an income producing order are quite slim. But then again, that happens sometimes as well."

"Some salespeople are inherently shy, and fear cold calling because they are unfamiliar with the facility or the individuals."

"I could understand that but I don't agree with it. A stranger is only someone that you haven't met yet. Will Rogers famous quote that "I never met a stranger I didn't like" rings true." Jerry throws that in to show Les that he knows his history, or that he has read some motivational books.

"OK, let's look at the process then, and let's assume you are calling on businesses."

"OK, go for it."

"You walk in the door and introduce yourself to the receptionist. The receptionist could receive you well, or act as though you interrupted the most important time of his or her day. Either could happen. You maintain politeness anyway."

"Right, I'm with you."

"Personally, I treat each cold call like a fact finding operation. Actually that is all it is anyway. If I get to see someone on an 'un-announced' stop, it's a bonus."

"Sure, I can see that as well." Jerry responds.

"I ask who the person is that would be involved with managing or purchasing the product or service I am providing. After they reveal that information I ask if that person is available."

"I can guess the results on that question."

"And you may be right. Nine out of ten times, they are un-available. It was somewhat unusual for us to meet that lady earlier this week on that cold call. However, it's perfectly fine either way. I will usually have a couple more questions that are so basic the receptionist knows the answer. Usually it is regarding the person's schedule or best time to contact them. Usually I ask the best method to contact as well. I may even ask for a business card for that person."

"Why would the receptionist have their business card?" Jerry asks.

"Mainly because there are a lot of people that come in and ask for that person. Believe me, they go through the drill more times daily than they care to talk about."

"Then what do you do?" Jerry asks impatiently.

"Hold on dude, I'm getting there." Les responds chuckling.

"I always enter the facility with a business card and some type of literature about my services. Remember how we did it earlier in the week?"

"Yeah."

"Yes, just like that."

"Usually I staple them together. There is controversy about if it is best to staple or leave the business card loose. I want them to know my name, and as much about what I do as possible."

"I can see why."

"If they actually un-staple my business card from my brochure, it is a mini-win. It means they are doing something with my card other than tossing it with my literature. While they are un-stapling my card, they will subconsciously learn more about my company by seeing the brochure."

"So, what takes place? By the end of the day? Results, I mean." Jerry inquires.

"If I make 20 stops that day I usually meet 3 people face to face that could at some time purchase my products or services. That percentage of a face to face meeting on cold calling is about average."

"And the others?"

"11 individuals will probably never see my card or literature because the receptionist tossed it, or it got put into a stack that may never get reviewed."

"They keep the filter in place, what else?" Jerry keeps prodding.

"6 people looked at my stuff, and put it off to the side of their desk to actually research later, or toss it out on the next review. However they may subconsciously acknowledge that the material was hand delivered instead of mailed, depending on how the receptionist delivered it to them. I personally think it means more."

"Wow, you don't make it sound bad at all. I'm ready to do it tomorrow." Jerry enthusiastically remarks.

"You'll get your chance, don't worry."

"Also, when you are out making those calls...?" Les questions in a reminding fashion.

"Yes," Jerry responds.

"Remember, organization is one of the key elements to success in this profession. If you are an unorganized slob, and don't care about methods to improve, you will go away quick."

"Well, I'm not a slob, so I don't have to worry about that." Jerry exclaims.

"If you are a traveler Jerry, as you will be, you need a clean vehicle. Your vehicle is your remote office and it needs to be organized. Spend the time to organize your sales material, your quotes and especially your route. Even if it is not a routine route."

"I got that." Jerry nods.

"You must know where you are going, and how to get there."

"I'm sure GPS units have really taken the stress out of this."

"Oh yeah, they are very well worth any investment if you are a travelling sales person."

"Also, make sure your things in the car are anchored and lined up. A quick stop can turn your mobile office into an earthquake zone."

"I've notice that in your car Les. No clutter. It appears you have everything in the trunk. The only thing I saw unorganized in your trunk was the hard hat."

"That's because I was in too much of a hurry on the previous stop to secure it. I normally do."

"Oh I'm sure you do Les."

"You'll remember this. As you get out of your car, have your material in hand, as well as your mindset. Forget any negative things that are going through your mind. Your world exists at this point only about you, your walk into the building, and how you project yourself. Think about and have memorized what you are going to say in your greeting, and how you may respond to many different greetings."

Jerry responds, "Oh yeah, and remember the smile."

Les smiles.

"What about these memorized greetings? How important are they?"

"You mean scripts, as some people call them?"

"Whatever..." Jerry replies.

"I am not a fan of canned presentations, and I am offended when I am an audience member to someone reading their presentation from a piece of paper."

"Me too. I think it is such an insult. It's like they are saying that the audience wasn't important enough to put any effort toward."

"I think the same thing." Les answers back.

"However, when you are a professional sales representative and you get the chance to introduce your product or service to someone, you want to be intimately familiar with what you want to share with them. You may have their attention for just a microscopic amount of time. It is your goal to present as much information as they can comprehend."

"Isn't what you just said a contradiction to the golden rule of selling? To listen more than you talk?" Jerry asks, almost confused.

"We're talking about two totally different environments. On a greeting, you have a very brief window to help your recipient decide if you are worth their time to move you through to the next level."

"OK, that makes it a little clearer."

"Be overly courteous and polite. Controlled energy helps here as well, but don't talk fast, and listen carefully. If you have their attention, use it to present yourself in a professional manner. Again, a courteous manner."

"As you learn and memorize your material it will not even be a script. It will just be you talking and sharing information with others. When you know your material, the stress level disappears, and you can control much of your thoughts and actions."

"As you mentioned earlier this week, I can see how this will really help if you are interrupted."

"It's amazing what a little effort and planning will do to help you make it through the screening process with these gatekeepers." Les responds reassuringly.

"OK, now I've made it through the screening process and I am actually face to face with the correct person. What are your suggestions here?"

"When you get the chance to present your wares, or even get the chance to talk with a key person, you want to retain as much of the conversation discussed as possible. And, don't ever think that taking notes during a meeting will insult your prospective customer. Even if you have to stop the conversation, it is usually looked at as taking a very sincere interest in them. Most prospective customers will be flattered if done right."

"I can see that," Jerry responds.

"Don't however turn it into a tedious survey. If your customer is interacting in meaningful conversation with you while this process is taking place, you are doing it right. If you are the only one talking, and they are just answering your questions, it's not a sales call, it's an embarrassment,"

"Really?" Jerry asks.

"Absolutely. Always try and keep the conversation equal with shared talking and listening."

"Remember my note taking? Your notes are your guaranteed memory. Document them the best you can."

"Give me some input on follow up calls then." Jerry requests, giving Les the opportunity to complete the whole topic.

"Follow up calls can be done right or done wrong."

"Really, now that makes a lot of sense, huh?" Jerry then looks at Les with a silly look on his face."

"Yeah, that's quite an intelligent statement." Les laughs.

"Combined with the documented knowledge that you left with on your first call you may really be able to help your prospective customer on the second call. And, just for the record you are required to make the second call."

"OK, I remember the Cardinal Rule."

"This one however can be tricky. It shouldn't be a cold call. It needs to be scheduled. The prospective customer needs to be advised that you have found a solution for them. If in fact you have. If you haven't, you have nothing to tell them other than thank you for their time. And that could be the reason for the second call."

"I guess, if nothing else we are building rapport with each other." Jerry comments.

"Quite possible."

Les continues.

"The concept of the follow up is simple. First question is do you have a reason to follow up?"

"You can follow up for many reasons but a few of the most vital are:"

"Can you help these people, or do you just want to get to know them? Both are valid reasons."

"Your first call is research based."

"Do they have needs or an interest you can help with?"

"Can you provide better products or services than they are currently getting?"

"Will dealing with your company be a benefit to them?"

"If the answer is yes to any of those questions, it is your job as a representative for your company to get that help implemented."

"But I may need more information to determine the answers to some of those questions?" Jerry comments.

"That is the challenge. That is your challenge."

"If you determine that you can help, you need to document precisely your solution. You need to have it designed and organized in as many ways as you can as to how the help can be implemented."

"Back to the organization thing."

"It is pinnacle!"

"You then go back and present your methods on helping them. If you have determined that you can't help, let them know, and move on."

"Just like that, move on?" Jerry questions.

"Probably." Les responds.

"Jerry, keeping this process going is a big challenge."

"I can see how it could be."

"You have to maintain passion and an accomplishable, measureable process flow consistently."

"What do you mean an accomplishable, measureable process flow?"

"Think of it like this. When one goes out and digs a hole in the field it means something to that person. When they leave at the end of the day, they can observe what they have accomplished."

"So...."

"That is what we as a workforce rely on. Either seeing our accomplishments, or being recognized in some way for that accomplishment. But for now, I'm just talking about seeing an accomplishment."

"I'm going a bit off topic now, but hang in there, I'll be back."

"I'm not going anywhere."

"A visible accomplishment was one of the things that companies lost when they automated their data processing system."

Jerry is shaking his head as he is not seeing where Les is taking this particular 'yarn.'

"Individuals were accustomed to manually go over stacks of paper and edit, audit, or something. They started with a stack of 'un-dones' in the morning, and could look at a huge stack of 'dones' at the end of the day.' Now we bring in a computer. The data gets crunched, the files don't even stick around before they are uploaded, or sent via email to someone else. There is no visual sign of accomplishment. Years back when automation first entered the scene, this was a tough adjustment for many task driven human document processors."

"Of course, automation eliminated a host of paper processing positions, and it boiled down to the ones that could type or keypunch every day with no 'paper stacking' separation anxiety. Keypunch cards for data information provided at least a stack of something that was accomplished. But then punch cards went away and it's where we are today."

"Now, back to my original point. Making sales calls every day is tedious if not created and organized in a way to feel an accomplishment. Multiple phone calls, waiting for callbacks, leaving messages, and not to mention driving to appointments that never happen. These all are efforts, that are hard to visually comprehend as accomplishments."

"So what happens?"

"Two scenarios are most likely to happen."

"You will hit it hard trying to contact as many people as possible. You will most likely neglect the organizational approach. Your efforts will start to produce activity, however, you will be lost in a maze of confusion or doubt because you didn't prepare, or plan or organize."

"Or, you will spend more time planning and organizing than making calls and you will produce fewer results."

"It makes sense, Les. It really does. What do you do?"

"The key is to find a happy medium, and constantly revisit how your system is working. Constantly analyze your methods, and look for ways to improve for efficiency, as well as results."

"I know that you have probably heard this analogy before, but I am going to torment you with it again."

"What's that?"

"Think of an airplane in route to a specified destination. Once in the air the winds are constantly trying to blow the plane off course. The rudder has to always be adjusted. It's the same way in this business. Always check, and recheck your methods to determine if they are effective. Just because it worked last year, doesn't mean it is the most efficient method for this year."

"I get it Les, and yes I have heard it before."

CHAPTER SEVENTEEN

"Jerry, have you ever heard anyone say that something is so easy, even a monkey can do it?"

"Oh yeah, and in some circumstances it is true." Jerry responds.

"What if you heard it about a profession that you were in, maybe like the sales arena?"

"Currently, it wouldn't be offensive, but if I were a veteran sales person it may sting a little bit."

"I've heard it and it has stung." Les states, but there are some parts to the analogy that may be true. Do you want to hear them?"

"Sure, where else am I going?"

Both men laugh.

"I am a firm believer that consistent, professional exposure to prospective customers will eventually produce sales. I would also say that in my opinion it's guaranteed."

"OK."

"There are many key words in that statement, but the first one I want to address is the word exposure. Exposure alone is a start."

"The next word that must be brought into this topic is timing. Timing is crucial as well."

"Do we guess at what the best time is for our exposure to these prospects, or how is that calculated?" Jerry asks.

"First of all we must know a bit about the industry and most importantly the buying cycles. Those are fairly simple things to find out. You do it just by asking."

"Are prospective customers always willing to share with you as a prospective vendor what the buying cycles are?"

"Usually, yes. That is of course if you present yourself as credible. Genuinely credible and ethical individuals can learn most anything from a prospective customer."

"Hmm," Jerry is thinking.

"Don't misunderstand, I don't mean that they do it in a manipulative way either."

"I understand."

"Now let's get back to looking at a monkey."

"We can train a monkey to visit customers. Someone would have to drive them around of course and you would have to arm it with sales brochures."

"Sure."

"While the monkey is there it can entertain them. Maybe even keeping their attention for a short while."

"Eventually the prospective customer will call your company to purchase something. One of your customer service people will give them the information that they need."

"That could be a very long 'eventually.'" Jerry states.

"True, but the initial premise is that monkeys can do things to generate business."

"OK. Not totally down with it, but I'll keep listening."

"So now, let's reevaluate our purpose as human salespeople."

"We can drive ourselves to the customer. Monkeys can't do that."

"We could entertain the customer, if the customer needs entertaining. We could find something entertaining to do."

"We can educate the customer by asking questions and providing answers. Monkeys can't do that."

"So, what's the conclusion to this particular twisted lesson, Les?" Jerry says smirking.

"I guess the lesson to the 'monkey' analogy is that most any type of interaction can produce sales in time. But, the human element brings so much more to the arena if done with any type of consistency and professionalism."

"OK, I can buy that."

"You know, we've talked a lot about sales calls and interacting with people, but one device hasn't been discussed much. Why?" Jerry asks.

"What device is that?" Les responds.

"The telephone."

"A telephone is a very good tool to save you time and money prospecting for customers. But, it is not as impacting as a personal face to face visit."

"I agree Les, completely. I have qualified so many people by using a telephone. It's how I previously made a living, remember?" Jerry continues.

"I know, and when done right, the telephone can be a very powerful tool." Les responds.

"Jerry, then what are your thoughts on using the phone?"

"Les, my mindset is a bit different than many if you are talking about making discovery phone calls. I use one main approach."

"OK." Les responds.

"It is the approach that I am calling just to find out something and would they have the time to point me in the right direction. Communicated correctly, you can be delivered directly to the correct person."

"Exactly," Les again agrees.

"No one wants to, or has time to be grilled over the phone, or blasted at about something they don't care about. You need to be empathetic with their time and attention. If they truly sense you care and respect their time, most will answer a few questions for you."

"That's right, because much of it is all about communicating empathy."

"You do realize that you are coming in with a great advantage over many rookie salespeople, don't you?"

"What do you mean?" Jerry asks.

"You can use the telephone like a precision instrument. It can and should save you personally a ton of time managing your sales territory. Not everyone has your experience in that arena. You would be surprised how many people are intimidated by the telephone."

"OK, we'll count that as a win for me," Jerry says, drawing a close to the telephone topic so he can ask another question.

Jerry is finalizing his notes on that topic and makes his familiar checkmark.

"Here is a topic that I have been avoiding, but it's the last one on my list."

"What is it?" Les asks concerned.

"Goals. I don't do them." Jerry states candidly and waiting for Les to slap him.

"I'll tell you something Jerry. I don't do them like I should either."

Jerry is shocked.

"Yeah, sure. You squeegee your car windows off in the hotel parking lot. You make notes after every call like a newspaper reporter. Don't tell me you don't make goals."

Jerry doesn't believe what Les just said.

"Honest. Do you know how much emphasis is put on goal setting? Tons. I think that goal setting gets so much 'play' in the sales arena, and so much is written about it, no one could do it perfect.....then again what is 'perfect?'"

Jerry is sure there is more to be said and as normal, Les continues.

"That being said, I will tell you that it is very important. And it is something that we all need to work on."

"OK."

"Jerry, getting to know you like I have, it is imperative that you use some type of goal setting procedure. It's a given that your quota goals will be provided for you. Those are inherited, but you could make magic happen if you develop goal setting habits early on."

"Do you think so Les?"

"Yes, and here is why." Les is starting to inhale and wind up to one of his famous gold plated beliefs.

"Just write down what you want to accomplish. Did you hear me?"

"Yeah."

"What did I say?" Les asks in almost a sarcastic tone.

"You said to write down what I want to accomplish. You just said it. What are you doing, testing me for Alzheimer's?" Jerry is joking.

"I know you heard it. What do you think is the key word in that statement? Take a guess."

Les is watching Jerry reviewing in his mind, now with more thought.

"Accomplish." Jerry states.

"That's an important word, but that isn't the one that drives the concept."

"Then its 'I.'" Jerry tosses out as he is looking out the window not to make eye contact with Les.

Chapter Seventeen

Les is observing Jerry. Jerry won't look at Les. Les is finally catching on to Jerry's little game.

"You weasel! You're messing with me aren't you?"

Jerry turns around and is grinning at Les.

"You have played those games with me enough on this trip, I thought I would at least try and get one on you." Jerry is laughing.

"Les, I know how important it is to write stuff down. It's like a task list. It gets done if you write it down….oh yeah, I remember and prioritize." Jerry looks at Les out of the corner of his eye.

"You're right. But the thing about writing goals down is that when you write down a goal, it somehow changes the way you think and do things."

"And I'll take it one step further. It almost changes the universe for you as well. But you have to keep reviewing your goals. You must keep reading what you wrote."

"I've always thought that I should be more proactive in that area, I really have. I just have a hard time taking goal setting to the extremes that most people do." Jerry remarks.

"I guess it all depends on what your priorities are, and how much commitment you intend to put forth when you start out."

"You know Jerry, you are at a spot in your life as well as this new career where some simple goal planning could really help you. I would say in the next couple of months you should sit down and write up some concepts that you would want to shoot for. You probably don't want to set too specific of work related goals, at least until you know more about what you are getting involved in. Does that make any sense?"

"Yeah, it does actually. I could start with writing some personal goals, now that I am on this career path. I may not be real familiar about this career as of yet, but I sure as heck understand all of my personal situations. I could set up some goals for some personal improvements immediately."

"Well then. As my friend Mike told me after we raised my car up on the lift that dramatic afternoon, 'get at it.'"

Both men snickered.

The drive back to the ContainPro complex was quicker than normal. Les and Jerry stopped in to visit Rudy and Luna, and yes, they each had one of Luna's sweet rolls. Jerry wasn't disappointed.

"Les, again this has been a real pleasure for me. I am so optimistic about my future, and I am excited to be working with people of your caliber. It has been a great trip. Thank you again for all of the help."

"I'm glad I can be involved in your initial development Jerry. I've always wondered what I would tell a new guy coming into our organization. I hope I wasn't too outspoken."

"It was perfect. It was just perfect."

"We should probably go check in with Dirk and give him a debriefing. He's usually available this time in the afternoon."

Chapter Seventeen

CHAPTER EIGHTEEN

Saturday morning seemed like it would never get there. Les and Cindy wanted to know as much about the Winman's situation as they could. They needed to know.

Les was really experiencing mixed emotions about the path that he and Cindy's life had turned onto. He was still in shock from hearing about Frank. Frank was a great friend. He and Les had shared a lot of good times as well as successes together. He remembers the time that he had broke a long standing sales record at Morphics. Frank was his biggest cheerleader during the year. He personally arranged a party and got the whole group together after work one night to celebrate Les's success.

Frank held their friendship very close. He had also been a very dedicated and focused sales professional. Not quite the caliber that Les was, but very much a standout for the company.

Frank's past was a bit different than Les's. He had a traumatic childhood which led him to be on his own at age 16. Frank found friends where ever he could and at times this didn't prove beneficial.

He grew up in an age when smoking appeared to be a common way to increase your public maturity image. He smoked for most of his life but had just recently quit. It was a direct order from his doctor.

For many years Les and Frank were like brothers bonded at the hip. They discussed daily the ups and downs of their careers. When one of them would get an "atta-boy" the other would be the first to hear about it. When one of them would take a hit from a superior, or witness a pathetic demeaning sales meeting, the other one was there to put ointment on the wound.

Les and Frank's friendship made the ups and downs of an unpredictable sales career tolerable. Their wives could only understand a small portion of what they experienced daily, but when they talked amongst themselves it was always worthwhile. Few people find friends that they can team up with within a sales organization. A typical salespersons life surprisingly is one of a loner. They usually don't let many inside of their personal lives.

Cindy Brigham was very good at supporting Les through his ups and downs as well. She was a model wife and mother. She raised her children well while Les lived out his travelling sales career. She listened intently with as much empathy or joy possible through his ups and downs.

The Brigham's had discussed this business venture in depth. Initially the biggest challenge that they could imagine was how Les was going to tolerate being in an office each day.

Les discussed this exact topic with Frank as well. Frank's response was that Les could design his position in that company any way he wanted to. If the job required periodic onsite trips to a customer's location, Les better be ready to travel. One of the caveats of Les assuming the CEO position was that Cindy could now go with him. This was a strong bonus for her and she was looking forward to the travel.

Sarah Winman was certainly not a dormant housewife. She had spent much of her childhood as well as her adult life working closely, and often right beside her father.

Being Frank's wife for over 35 years provided its challenges as well. The Winman's had no children.

Frank had a wondering eye for the lady's. Sarah knew it as well. Their agreement was that Frank could admire from a distance but if he got too close to anyone he would be harmed severely. Sarah's brothers were watching out for their little sister as well and Frank figured they would just kill him and dispose of his body if he ever went astray. Rich and Rod Layman lived on the edge and liked playing with sharp objects.

Unfortunately for Frank Winman, he didn't always think things through. On a business trip several years ago he got to know a hotel desk attendant just a little too well. It was during a time that he and Sarah were dealing with some personal issues between themselves. The desk attendant knocked on his door one night after her shift and he let her in. She was terminated the next morning when she was getting into her car. That morning Frank Winman started thinking about his own mortality.

Luckily Frank's secret was Frank's secret. The only one that knew about it was himself, the dismissed desk attendant and Les Brigham. Even though Les will die with that bit of information going undisclosed, it did tarnish Les's overall image of his close friend. But being the allies that they were for each other, Les has let it go and Frank Winman has been a model husband ever since.

The telephone rang that Saturday morning just as the two had arranged. Both couples had their phones on speaker mode so it was like a group discussion only without being together.

"Frank, we are very concerned," were the first words out of Cindy's mouth.

It was quiet for a short time on the other end and Sarah responded.

"Cindy, we are as well and have been for a while. I'm hoping that we can give you all the details this morning so you will feel better."

Sarah continued.

"You guys both know that we were certainly not attempting to be deceptive regarding Frank's health. You do know that, don't you?" Sarah asked in a tone hoping for reassurance and acceptance of their actions.

"We know that sweetie," Cindy responded. We are just very concerned and need to know what you know about the future."

They could hear Frank clearing his throat in the background.

"The prognosis is quite dim, I'll tell you that. I am following the doctor's orders by getting my affairs in order."

There were many segments of silence in today's conversation.

Frank continued.

"I've got lung cancer. And it's spreading. I've chosen not to deal with the suffering and agony of certain treatments so we have chosen the path that will give us the best quality of life. I don't want to be a burden and I definitely will not be a long term vegetable."

Les was hearing this news and was shaking a bit. He wanted to yell at Frank for smoking all those years but felt it wouldn't accomplish anything. This wasn't the time to be mad at Frank, it was the time to love him for who he was.

"I feel fine and have noticed no real signs of this thing hurting me as of yet. However it could start tomorrow. That's the unknown."

"The good news is that money isn't a worry. Not only is Sarah taken good care of through her dad's enterprises, my life insurance will give her plenty of spending money."

Chapter Eighteen

"You know I'd give it up….." Sarah started to comment.

"We know believe me, we know." Cindy interrupted.

"Frank, what do you think our time frame is for completion of the legal crap? I want to spend as much time as I can with you before…" and then Les stopped talking.

"Dude, you can kiss your folks at ContainPro goodbye today if you want to. I can put you on an interim salary that will make you both happy and you can start working beside me. Not only would I welcome that plan, I would suggest it."

Sarah added. "Cindy, you can hang out here any time you want to as well. I really want our small group of employees to get to know you. I really think that you will get along with them great."

These were the words that Les fantasized about hearing. He never imagined he would be the recipient of this type of offer.

Another caveat for the Brigham's was that they were going to be able to move back home. The business was in their home town. The same town that they moved from three years prior when Les joined the ContainPro team.

"Let me work on that exit concept over the weekend. I want to plan it right so Dirk doesn't lose it. Crap, I just start to get along with the damn guy, just starting to break down the barriers, and I'm running out the door. Why does it always have to be bittersweet?"

Both couples chuckle.

"Life isn't simple man, we both know that." Frank responds.

Sarah jumps in with some information.

"By the way we have had a group meeting at the office. The entire group knows of our plans. They know that some people very close to us will be taking over the company. They are anxious to meet you both."

"And, one more thing. Our employees are all long term folks. Some of them were personal friends of my dad's. They are aware of Frank's health, but only a select few know all of the details."

Sarah continues.

"Because of the revenue we produce, and of our unique niche some of those people make a very generous income. They also live and breathe that business as well. They look at that company as their own company, but not one of them would be able to, or want to take it over and they all know it. I say that to reassure you that they are looking forward to an amiable boss that knows how to work with them and not over them."

"You know how I feel about that scenario Frank. There will not be any power struggles."

"Not worried at all buddy. We have a lot of fun there so far, and I know you will too." Frank agrees.

"OK then. Are you guys OK, Cindy are you doing all right with all of this?" Frank asks.

"Absolutely. I can't wait to see you guys and hug the stuffing out of you, and we will make that very soon. You both are in our prayers."

"I'll have a game plan together by Monday morning and I'll call you or email you with the details. I'll be ready by then to prepare a two week working scenario to present to Dirk, and help him adjust. They may try to talk Ken out of retiring so quick and put Jerry in my territory. I'll be leaving before Ken now. Who knows what they'll do?"

"They are going to lose a great guy, but I will promise you that you will not once look back with regret. I'll repeat that right before I tell Sarah goodbye with my last dying breath."

"Don't be so damn dramatic Frank. I'm not ready to cry over you yet, or say goodbye so just leave those poignant, tear jerking comments for later. OK?" Les is laughing.

"OK, but you do have to promise me that you will erect a shrine for me somewhere in the facility."

"I'll make you a shrine alright. It will be in the form of an outhouse and we'll put it in the back lot by the loading docks. I'll get a plaque made and nail it over the door. It will have your name on it."

Both couples are in hysterics at this point.

"I know I could count on you Les. That's why I love you."

The conversation ended shortly after that as both parties needed to dig into their Saturday task list. Yes, the prioritized one.

Monday morning came and the first thing Les did was to sit down with Dirk Youngblood and reveal his future. Dirk took it well and was almost envious of Les and Cindy.

Les's exit plan made sense to Dirk just as Les had hoped. That was just how Les was. He hated to inconvenience anyone.

"Please stay in touch with us Les. You have helped re-vitalize not only this entire sales force but provide unconditional help for me with little reward. You are one of the best of the best."

The two men shook hands in Dirks office for one of the last times.

Chapter Eighteen

CONCEPT SUMMARIES

The following topics are general summaries and opinions that were discussed in the book. Decide if they are useable for you.

DIET AND HEALTH

This is where you make it or break it as far as your own body. Try to look at your health as you would look at your own car. You really can't get from place to place without it. And, when you drive it into a customer's parking lot wouldn't it be nice if it was in decent condition. It says a lot about how you live and think.

KEY ATTRIBUTES FOR SUCCESS

Although this topic could be a book in itself, I feel that in order to be successful in this profession you must have at a minimum the following traits:

1. Enthusiasm with tenacity
2. Organizational skills
3. Product knowledge
4. Intelligence with common sense
5. Honesty
6. Integrity

SALESPEOPLE. WHAT ARE THEY

Salespeople are individuals that are armed daily with solutions for individuals or companies. Their job is to find those in need of those solutions and secure an agreement with those individuals to procure them.

TRUST

Without trust, you have a very tough process ahead. It is like clearing the land before you can build a road.

CLOSING SALES

Closing a sale is nothing more than creating a functional purchase agreement with an individual or company. You have provided a strong enough sense of value in yourself and your product or service that the customer will provide you with money in exchange.

A personal note: We often hear from our management teams, "Let us know what we can do to help you 'close' the business. "What I would like to hear become the standard message is, "Let us know how we can help you 'earn' the business." I think it would create a different dynamic.

PERSONAL UNIQUENESS

This is the perception by someone else that you are different. The goal is to secure that perception of uniqueness in a positive fashion.

EXPERIENCE, KNOWLEDGE & CONFIDENCE

For beginners, these three topics almost fall into place in this order. Your experience will give you knowledge, and your knowledge will give you confidence. All three are cornerstones of your success.

THE VALUE OF YOUR PRESENCE

This is different than personal uniqueness. This is how you are valued by your customers by being in their presence. If you had no interest in them, they would probably have no interest in you. It would also create no value in their eyes toward you.

SERVICE

Service goes beyond your looks, your style, and all of the other building blocks. Service is the actual action that you provide for, and on behalf of your customer.

EMPATHY

Empathy is sitting beside your customer and feeling the emotions that they are feeling. It is about you understanding and feeling all of the circumstances to the events that are taking place with any of their given situations.

HONESTY AND CANDIDNESS

Honesty is a given. Candidness or revealing facts that are not well known must be used with intelligent judgment. There are many times that do not require everything to be revealed.

PRODUCT PROGRAMS

Product programs, or promotions as some call them are not designed for every customer you have. You as a representative to them, based on your knowledge of their needs should have a fair understanding as to who will benefit from provided promotions and programs.

SELF PROMOTION

This is not to be confused with bragging or boasting. Self Promotion is about creating a true and factual image of yourself as a knowledgeable resource for those you deal with.

LISTENING

Although we all say we are good at it, and do it often, it is a tough ongoing challenge for many. Especially if we are motivated by what we represent. This is one concept that could and should be practiced consistently.

FIRST IMPRESSIONS

This is similar and goes along with the Health and Diet topic. Your appearance and your speech will speak so loudly as to whom you are, chances are you will not have to go into much detail.

SCRIPTS

I refer to scripts as practiced and rehearsed segments of introductory speech describing yourself, your company, or your products or services.

BUSINESS VS PERSONAL LIFE

The more you get involved with your career, these two will constantly collide. Try to develop the understanding of who you are at specific times and places. Practice that understanding.

QUOTA

Quota is a word that scares so many. It's like the big spacecraft that looms overhead and not knowing exactly what is coming out when the beam of light descends. So much emphasis is placed on quota within organizations it becomes almost a swear word. All it happens to be is a number that is required to achieve in order to receive certain monetary rewards, or unfortunately possibly retaining your present job. The downside is that it is also the number to blame if your performance didn't provide you with the results to meet it.

SALES SLUMPS

In the world of sales, you will encounter a slump. It can be feared or ignored. The best approach to dealing with a sales slump is to understand how it occurred, or why it is occurring, and design a proactive plan to change it.

CUSTOMER RELATIONSHIPS

What I am referring to here is the bond that you will develop with your customers. At times this may be considered the true payoff for choosing your career in sales. Choose your customer friendships wisely, and try to understand why they are in place.

FINANCES: BUSINESS & PERSONAL

Very briefly. Keep business and personal finances separate. Use separate credit cards and bank accounts.

INITIAL COMPENSATION PLANS AND PROCEDURES

Starting out in many sales careers, you could be offered a certain compensation amount for a limited period of time. This is offered to keep you solvent while building your sales territory and establishing yourself with your customer base. My only advice here is to see as many, do as much as you can, and get yourself established. Don't hold back. This is "full throttle" time.

PERSONAL BUDGETING FOR SALESPEOPLE

Income for salespeople can fluctuate. Just that scenario alone has kept many people from passing up a possibly fulfilling career in sales. My advice here is to create reserve accounts for major and definite expenditures. If you know you will need to spend a certain amount in the distant future, start putting aside proportioned amounts in a reserve savings account every month prior. Keep good records of what you spend your money on as well and review those amounts monthly. You will have meager months as well as lucrative months. Always prepare for the future.

ADD ON, OR SCANNING FOR ADDITIONAL SALES

Growing a territory is about finding more acceptable offerings to your customers. Don't settle for meager purchases, when they can benefit from buying additional things from you. Chances are that they won't volunteer what those are. You will have to ask what they are. Always keep your eyes open for what you see them using. They have to buy it somewhere. And if you sell it, create the desire in their eyes as to why they should buy it from you.

ATTITUDE

If you don't have the proper attitude you will have better luck trying to get water to burn with a match. Your attitude is your fuel. It's is what makes you move. It's what makes you talk. It's what makes you think. It's everything. Create a good attitude, and protect it like it is the blood in your veins.

INTEGRITY

Everyone may have a different definition of integrity but mine goes like this. Integrity is doing the right thing, regardless of what the benefits are. It is purely decisions based on good moral character with personal benefits not being considered.

PEERS

Choosing peers also goes along with leadership. Watch other people and learn from them. You don't need to model them, just learn and pull from their positive attributes the ones you find beneficial. Just because most of your team mates idolize a particular person has no bearing as to how you should feel about them.

TEAM HELPING

This will either be something that you understand, or ignore. Many salespeople are like individual islands. Their rewards are based on their paychecks. Their mindset is that "if I wanted to help everyone, I would have pursued a management career." Well rounded individuals help others on their team. It is appreciated by many, but by some it is overlooked.

MANAGERS AND GOALS

Dealing with managers is tricky. Many different types, and all with different agendas. Some managers want to know what your goals are so they can truly help you achieve them.

Other managers look at their positions as babysitters and are cued only by looking for your shortcomings. If you have a strong trusting relationship with your manager, by all means let them in as far as you feel comfortable.

PERSONAL INDEPENDENCE

The life of a salesperson can be a very lonely life. Many of us are very independent and actually could be considered 'loners' by many evaluations. We would struggle sitting in a cubicle only to eat at a given hour every day and following prompts like trained cattle. (Can you tell I am jaded?) Much like the personal friendships that you develop, your freedom and flexibility are omnipotent.

SETBACKS

Setbacks and sales go together. It's part of the life. Remember, you probably see as many people, and share as much business intimacy as your personal physician. You will experience bumps in the road. The only defense in dealing with a business or monetary setback is to pull your tenacity out of your back pocket and put it into play.

YOUR VALUE TO YOUR CUSTOMER

This is entirely your job. You must define your value, create your value, and subliminally exploit that value to your customer as well as yourself. If you struggle constantly with finding your personal value, chose another career. Your days are limited with this one.

COMPARTMENTALIZED THINKING

If you can grasp the concept of this, it will save your life. Not only in business but your personal life as well. The basis for success in this area is to be able to analyze issues that come along and keep them separate in their own unique place and time. Don't let an argument you had with your family member carry over to your customer. Realize where you are each day and time. Know your role and purpose then and there. Period.

ORGANIZATION/TASKS/PRIORITY

This is another life sustaining topic not limited to the arena of sales. If you struggle with organization please get help. If you are not analyzing your tasks and projects as well as setting a level of importance, start immediately. Research help if you must, because it is vital. Organization is vital.

CUSTOMER COURTESY

When you are with a customer, see the world in their eyes. Understand that you are not as important to them as their own customers. I realize that this is hard to accept, especially if you have developed a strong friendship. Do nothing to jeopardize, inhibit, or cause any type of disruption toward their customer. When you are at their place of business, you are "second string."

CREATIVE PROBLEM SOLVING

It is a simple process and it delivers huge rewards. Learn to sit quietly and concentrate on a particular question. Record answers that flash into your mind. Don't judge them, just record them. Try to do this regularly and for a set amount of time. Overcome the distractions and understand that your time during this process is catapulting you a long distance ahead of your competitors. Be sure and test the solutions that you deem acceptable.

HELPING OR SELLING?

People do like to buy things. We can't ignore that fact. However, most things are purchased to fulfill a need. It could be a physical need in the case of food. Or it could be a career need in the case of tools. The list goes on and on. Fulfilling a need is helping. The more you help, the more you receive. As much as people get a warm feeling by spending money, that warm fuzzy is multiplied when they are receiving true help as well.

KEY INDIVIDUALS

Understand the hierarchy of any business you call on. Know who the person is that makes the decisions to buy. Know who the person is that influences the person to procure your solutions. If you are building up a relationship with a person that can not influence anyone to purchase your offerings, I certainly hope you enjoy fishing together. You'll have lots of time to do it.

DEFINING SUCCESS

Someone asked me one time if I thought I was successful. From a career standpoint I felt I was. I enjoy my time performing my occupation. I enjoy my time at home with my family. The income provides us with the lifestyle we find quite acceptable. I sleep at night. I don't experience "Sunday Night Trauma." And I feel that I am providing a benefit to those I interact with on a professional level. If you set up a haphazard monetary income level, or a certain type of recognition level you feel you need to attain and label yourself unsuccessful until you hit it, I would be worried. But here again, motivation to attain success can be interpreted in many ways.

COLD CALLING

Cold calling is nothing more than making unarranged stops or unarranged phone calls at any given time. You can cold call existing customers as well, but my definition of cold calling is walking into doors you have never been in before and finding out who the folks are. You can later determine if you want to pursue them as a customer after you have done due diligence as to how you could work with them.

FOLLOWUPS

If you make a call on a prospective customer. If it gets you nowhere, and you neglect to attempt to find out more, pack it in. You are done. You may as well go drive down the street with your windows rolled down shouting your name and what you do. Your results will be about the same. It is a Cardinal Rule that if you make an unsuccessful call because of missing a person, or you didn't get the information you needed, you must make another call. Remember, it's a Cardinal Rule.

MAN VERSES MONKEY

The only reason I am even addressing this topic here is because I have heard so many times, "it is so easy, a monkey could do it." Well, the last time I checked a monkey couldn't talk. Few can drive cars safely. They can dial a telephone but after the dialing process they are pretty much sunk as far as intelligent communication. The last time I checked, intelligent, human communication is how successful business arrangements exist.

GOALS

Goals are mandatory for success! Without them, it takes a lot more time, a lot more money and a lot more patience Define some type of goal early. Goals should be written down and read regularly. Just the simple procedure of that alone will move you directly toward your desires.

Concept Summaries

SAMPLE QUESTIONS AND ANSWERS THAT YOU COULD EXPERIMENT WITH

The following documentation represents pseudo sections of my personal journal. These are the types of questions that I ask myself on a fairly consistent basis. It helps me re-adjust my mindset as well as uncover new solutions to current concerns.

What can I tell other salespeople about how to stay focused and win?

1. Understand who you are committed to and list why. This can be anything, or anyone. Most importantly is that you know who or what it is. Define it and write it down.

2. Create a sentence as to that commitment and read it everyday. A wall poster or note is good, but writing it down <u>in</u> something is better. It's an action that will become a habit. A good habit.

3. Mindset. Health and nutrition. Be aware of food and rest.

4. Set and define an Achievement Point. You need to know your destination. Define the steps. Walk the steps.

5. Create an Instruction Manual for your job. Create it for you as you want to and should do it. This is specifically for you. It shouldn't be applicable to anyone else.

6. Influence upon yourself. Be careful of what others say and what you believe in their comments.

List my empowering/positive emotions/situations.

1. Inner knowledge of who I am as a person.

2. My reputation amongst my team mates.

3. My reputation amongst my family.

4. Satisfaction.

5. Accomplishments.

6. My commitment to exercise and the history of that commitment.

7. Knowledge of my environment, family, work, spiritual related, and how available these positive elements are to me.

8. My ongoing, everyday opportunity, availability and permission to do what I need to do to accomplish harmony, peace and success.

What can I do immediately to secure my focus for the next 90 days?

1. Avoid being overwhelmed.

2. Document my daily activities. This will be done for review analysis purposes only.

3. Document my daily commitments.

4. Schedule those commitments.

5. Review those commitments.

6. Don't over commit.

7. Be aware of the statements, commitments I make just to make the sale.

8. Always remember that I set the pace. No one else.

9. Always remember that I set the schedule. No one else.

10. Keep exercising.

11. Create relaxation or meditation techniques.

12. Identify my "commitment groups:" i.e. Family, company, customers, etc.

13. Be proactive on follow-ups regardless of my preconceived thoughts.

14. Tune out the "whiners."

15. Put forth strong, honest effort and realize inner
    peace.

List my disempowering, painful emotions and patterns.

1. Frustration

2. Guilt, imposed by others.

3. Vulnerability

4. Not being in control of my own happiness.

5. Waiting for, or anticipating a problem or a conflict.

6. Boredom by routine.

7. Hanging onto a negative picture or event in history.

8. Constantly reanalyzing and reliving past conflicts.

9. Knowing that I have the ability at any moment in time to completely change my pattern, but not acting on it.

What could I do or think to prevent negative reacting to new situations?

1. Stay focused on a picture in my mind that I am observing the events from a neutral perspective.

2. Keep exercising.

3. Start again and schedule meditation time.

4. When searching for things to say, search for the positive side of the 'page.' Stating negative remarks only draws a dark, stagnant cloud over my presence.

5. I have excellent capabilities to steer my mental path. Don't allow it to steer itself.

6. I must constantly steer the course of a positive focus.

7. When 'mental trauma' arises, look at it quickly and go through a quick checklist.

   a. What time of day is it?
   b. Have I eaten? Calorie depletion?
   c. Is this truly a battle that I am supposed to be involved with?
   d. Is it out of my control?
   e. Will thinking about it over and over provide peace?
   f. Who needs to give me reassurance to move on?
   g. Learn to 'switch' and 'move on.'

When I am totally overwhelmed, and need re-assuring thoughts to re-center myself, I read this.

My job is not 100% of who I am.

My job is my occupation, not my life.

I owe the company I work for, effort, dedication and focus, in return for an income.

I do not owe the company I work for, self-induced stress by feelings and fear of inadequacy.

My spirit, my integrity, and my character direct me.

My existence is my choice of "paths" or "environments of my mind." The hot, bumpy, dusty, noisy, uncomfortable path that I at times find myself on, should only be a detour back to a more efficient and healthy paved path, instead of the route I choose for the full trip.

No one is going to, or would I want them to engrave "He gave his life to his company" on my gravestone, or my urn of ashes.

If this is a desolate day, think of the people that I love, and all of those that love me, for there are many. They are in fact my only true reason for existence.

If by some very rare chance that life is really "only one trip through the salad bar" then I've got to start using more than one plate.

It appears that society is in the same chaotic mindset. Spend more time searching for the odd ones, the ones that are not.

Take frequent "mini-mind" vacations everyday, then go back and re-read this list.

If the company I work for, closed its doors, or disappeared tomorrow, who would I be?

Don't overindulge! Except with love and compassion….in fact, find my way of interpreting and practicing the latter.

Pick someone every week, to acknowledge, or say something encouraging to, like my close friends and family do for me.

Every person that I talk with today will have about the same amount of issues to deal with. Thiers are just different variations of mine. Even those facing mortality, or financial ruin, give each of those issues involuntary, constant and obsession of thought.

We all acquire a unique perspective on our lives and our existence. Our self-inflicted frustration comes from thinking that we are "on-center" and "they" are "off.'" That brain of theirs had human influence from the time they took their first breath, just like ours. Absolutely, no one is wrong as to how they think. Thinking is not a right-wrong concept. It is merely a perspective. It may differ from ours, and at times dramatically. Instead of getting "hacked" and feeling that that person is wrong, we should think, "That viewpoint definitely differs from mine," and at that instant, the analysis of that person regarding that issue should end. Only harm will come if we re-visit and hold on to the "right-wrong" concept.

All of my perceived conflicts are merely puzzles. If I don't particularly care for puzzles, I need to find ways to adopt a tolerance for them. All of these daily "puzzles" have solutions. My greatest satisfaction should be from developing superior "triage" skills early, regarding every puzzle. Triage defined as:

a. How much attention does this puzzle deserve?
b. What will be the effect on my peace of mind, if I choose not to find a solution to this puzzle?

What information can I document right now, that will help me complete my day today with a peaceful feeling of satisfaction?

I choose to block my day in hours and life from block to block. Build in some flexibility, and don't live and die by this "block of time" concept, but treat it like it warrants very high importance.

Re-read this material often.

LaVergne, TN USA
03 August 2010
191944LV00001B/7/P